Island Conversion

The Transition of a Gaelic Poet
from Sceptic to Believer

Myles and Margaret Campbell

The Islands Book Trust

Published in 2011 by The Islands Book Trust

www.theislandsbooktrust.com

ISBN: 978-1-907443-25-1

British Library Cataloguing in Publication Data. A CIP record for this book can be obtained from the British Library.

Typeset by Erica Schwarz
Printed and bound by Martins the Printers, Berwick upon Tweed
Cover design by Prepress Projects, Perth

The Islands Book Trust
Ravenspoint Centre
Kershader
South Lochs
Isle of Lewis
HS2 9QA
Tel: 01851 880737

Contents

Contents

Foreword

This is a very different book from any yet published by the Islands Book Trust, and a few words of explanation are in order.

The aim of the Book Trust is to further understanding and appreciation of the history and culture of Scottish islands. This normally takes the form of talks and publications which examine various aspects of the history of the islands, based on documentary records or oral history. We have also published creative writing and poetry where there is a link to a book or an historical event, and accounts of the cultural life of the islands either in the past or present. A theme which runs through much of our work is the different perspective on historical and cultural events from islanders themselves compared with those who are looking at island life from the outside.

Religion, and a belief in supernatural forces more generally, have played and still play a fundamentally important part in the culture of the Hebrides. Indeed, many would say that this is one of the dimensions which make island life and history distinctive. Certainly, Christianity has had a huge impact on Gaelic communities in the islands, and the views of islanders on religious matters, whether in the Catholic areas or in the Presbyterian areas, have for at least two centuries been an important and sometimes discordant influence on religious and intellectual development in Scotland.

To simplify, there has for many centuries been a greater predisposition in the Hebrides than on the mainland of Scotland, particularly in the large urban areas, to seek explanations of the world through a belief in supernatural phenomena. This is clear, for example, in Martin Martin's illuminating account of customs and beliefs in 'the Western Islands of Scotland' first published in 1703, and in the many expositions of 'Second Sight' which have followed. While it suited Martin's modernising Protestant agenda to heap scorn on practices he dismissed as 'Papist superstitions', there can be little doubt that a belief in the supernatural, through a transcendent God and the revealed truth of the Bible, was central to the success of the evangelical Presbyterian Revival which swept through many island communities in the first half of the 19th century.

Even today, a rejection of materialistic values and secular scientific explanations of the natural world is still a potent and distinctive force in the Hebrides. This is expressed particularly through the Churches, although this view is increasingly being threatened by the powerful agencies of the outside world, whether through the media or the growing number of 'incomers' to Hebridean societies who have been brought up in quite different cultures.

It is interesting to speculate on why this longstanding characteristic of Hebridean culture and society should have developed and survived. Part of the reason may be the challenges of living in a relatively hostile environment of infertile rocks and frequent storms, and the all-pervading influence of the sea – conditions which emphasise that important aspects of daily life are often outwith human control. And of course, once cultural patterns have become established, they will tend to be perpetuated, at least to a degree, through transmission mechanisms such as the family, community institutions, and the teachings of the Church.

I believe that the story told by Myles and Margaret Campbell in this book is inextricably linked to their island upbringing and cultural background, to the extent that it is unlikely to have been written in these terms by people less familiar with the traditional 'world view' of island societies . It is a very personal story, and one which honestly seeks to understand and interpret the events they have experienced and the conflicting intellectual and religious ideas to which they have been exposed. The fact that Myles is a well-known and very good Gaelic poet adds to the interest of the story. I am delighted that the text has been supplemented by so many of Myles' beautiful poems – in Gaelic and English – which add substantially to the appreciation of his personal testament.

Finally, I am clear that the ideas put forward by Myles and Margaret are worthy of respect. The Book Trust do not necessarily share the views of any of their authors, but we do think it valuable and instructive to consider different interpretations, whatever their perspective. This is a serious and thought-provoking account of a subject at the heart of island history and culture, and I am very pleased that we have been able to provide a platform for its publication, dissemination, and discussion.

John Randall
Chairman
The Islands Book Trust

April 2011

Introduction

1

Both authors' roots are in the Hebrides, Inner and Outer, and that fact alone has an important bearing on how we came to faith. Margaret's parents came from Breasclete, Isle of Lewis, and were brought up in the Free Presbyterian Church, as was Margaret herself. In chapter 2, she tells a little about her early upbringing on the island until she left for Inverness to train as a nurse when she was seventeen. She returned to the islands after some nineteen years and worked in Lewis for a number of years and in Benbecula with the Ministry of Defence. There, her nursing duties meant regular stays on St Kilda.

Unlike Margaret, my parents came from separate islands, my father from Ness in Lewis and my mother from Staffin in Skye. They both belonged to the Free Church of Scotland. My father was a missionary in the Church and at that time, in the 50s and 60s, it meant the Church could move him to a new congregation, as need arose, every few years. As a result, as a child I experienced life in different places and different islands, namely Skye and Lewis. Until the age of sixteen, I lived in Staffin, Uig (Skye), Borve (Lewis), Waternish, Staffin, Glenelg and Achmore (Lewis). From Glenelg, I attended Portree High School and stayed in the hostel during term time.

Staying in these different places gave me a good feel for the culture, especially the religious culture, of the islands. I heard hundreds of sermons from tens of ministers during my childhood years, as did Margaret. In a sense, we both rebelled, but the rebellions were very different. When Margaret left Lewis at 17, she stopped going to church and her religion fell away by default, as it were. Mine was an intellectual rebellion. I was interested in ideas and questioned the intellectual basis of the preaching I heard. As explained in the body of the book, it was going to be a very long time before I came to believe in the Christian religion.

On Facebook, I say that I'm a catholic with a small 'c' and it's true that I have no time for division in the Christian churches. I became a member of the Free Church, not because I have a great faith in churches, but because I have a faith in Christ and I wanted to show that faith in some way. For me Christ is truly universal, not sectarian or tribal. I really believe that everyone who believes in the Apostles' Creed should be in the same church. Looked at from outside, the present divisions are a disincentive to faith. Surely, they are sinful and a reproach to the Christ the churches worship.

2

The book is in two parts. Part 1 is a prose account of how Margaret and I met, separated, and eventually came together again and married. It is also the story of my struggle with faith. Part 2 is a Gaelic poem-sequence based on our experiences and with English translations.

There are two great strands in the way people have approached the idea of God. He is transcendent and unknowable, something totally other, or he is a God who is the intimate of the soul, a God who reveals himself to people. Many seekers after God could only speak of God by saying what he was not. Such was the anonymous author of *The Cloud of Unknowing* in the 14th century. For there is always the danger that in saying 'God is that' or 'God is this' we create our own idols. There is the danger that we create God in our own image.

We were aware of these dangers when writing this account for it is a very personal story. There is the obvious danger of claiming too much for personal experience. In what happened to us the subjective and the objective merge. Yes, it is the story of transcendence, a reality which is totally other. And yet a reality which appears to communicate with individuals at an incredibly personal level.

It is the story of a sceptical poet coming to believe in a supernatural explanation of the world rather than a naturalistic one. My wife, Margaret, was a believer and a Christian when I met her for the second time (because of a dream she had) in the year 2000. We had met 36 years previously in 1964. In the intervening period we had lost touch, gone our separate ways, married other people, divorced (in my case) and Margaret had become a widow.

The story has two main strands. One is the account of how we met again after so many years, of our marriage, and the unusual events that have happened since. The other strand is the story of my struggle with intellectual doubts and how they were eventually resolved. I promised myself as a teenager to find out the truth about life. Little did I know at the time where the search would lead.

Reductionism, naturalism, the scientific point of view, a dismissal of the possibility of a supernatural explanation – are they not the staples of the materialist world view? For many people in Europe today it seems to be the default position. For a long time, this was also my perspective on reality. It is only in the last few years that I have become convinced that such a view is wrong. And I can quite honestly say that it is what we have experienced personally that has finally convinced me that there is a supernatural side to the world. The infinite, transcendent, the Other, Origin, God, call it what you will, can and does, we believe, communicate with human beings, however unbelievable such a claim might be for the sceptic. Perhaps it is through his agents, for example, angels that he communicates. Nevertheless, there is communication. Twenty years ago, I would have found such a claim unbelievable. The story of this book is the story of why we think such a claim can *rationally* be made.

The two strands, the personal story and the intellectual struggle, are intertwined and reinforce one another throughout the book as they have done throughout my life. It means, in Part 1 of the book, that there is also a dual style of writing – one that reflects the personal stories and one where I discuss my problems with belief, where I refer to writers and scholars and give references.

In Margaret's case, the path to faith was different and she tells her own story.

Myles Campbell
Margaret Campbell

Isle of Skye, February, 2011

Acknowledgements

Thanks are due to a number of people who have helped us in different ways in bringing this book to completion. It is not a book that fits easily into publishers' categories. It is not straight biography but a mixture of life story and apologetics and we are most grateful to The Islands Book Trust for taking the risk of publishing something that is somewhat different. John Randall has kindly written a foreword placing the book in the wider context of island religion.

Professor Donald MacLeod was kind enough to read the manuscript at a busy time in his life and made many valuable comments. This in no way implies that he endorses all that is said in the book, for example, the theology, but it was most helpful to get his comments and his acknowledgement that it was mine and Margaret's personal spiritual stories and had every right to stand as such. Dr Emilia Evancu, a Romanian scholar, was greatly supportive throughout the writing and she herself played a part in the story, as the reader will discover. Thanks to her also for reading and commenting on the manuscript. We are grateful to Dr Alastair McIntosh (author of *Soil and Soul: People versus Corporate Power*) and to the Rev. Archibald Black for reading the manuscript and for the positive responses and encouragement they gave to publishing the story.

Our grateful thanks also to Dr Meg Bateman of Sabhal Mòr Ostaig, UHI, and to my (Myles) son, Alasdair for reading the text, making valuable comments and pointing out some typographical errors. Any errors that remain are entirely our own.

And last, but certainly not least, our grateful thanks to our minister and spiritual mentor the Rev. John MacLean, who observed at first hand some of what we went through in the process of writing, and who, despite the unusual happenings in our lives, supported us all the way. As the reader will discover, he was also closely involved with some of the events that took place. Again a disclaimer is necessary. Although he read the manuscript and was very supportive, that in no way implies an endorsement on his part of the views, theological or otherwise, expressed in the book.

But he has encouraged us very much to tell our story and how God dealt with us.

PART 1

• 1 •

How it all started

M argaret and I have been married for only 8 years (I write in 2010), but we had met many years previously in Inverness when she was training to be a nurse in 1964 aged 17. I was 19 and worked as a wages clerk with the County Council. We had a brief relationship at the time for two or three months when she had had broken up with her steady boyfriend, whom she would later marry. She left me to go back to him and that was that. I never saw her again for 36 years. We were to meet again following a dream she had in the 1990s.

If it were not for that dream and the mark it left on her, it is most unlikely we would ever have met again. Subsequent events since our marriage have proved conclusively, at least to us, that all this was meant to happen. We have, as it were, been pushed by powers – I use the word advisedly, as the reader will discover – beyond us to come together again, to write this book and to tell this story. We, ourselves, sometimes find it hard to believe what happened to us, but the following is the truth as it occurred. As I explained in the introduction, there are two strands to the story, the external events which happened in our lives and the inner intellectual and spiritual changes which happened to both of us.

There were great changes in my intellectual beliefs. These happened over time and there were reasons why I changed my mind. Part of the story is how and why my world view changed from one based on naturalism to its opposite, that is, to a belief in the supernatural origin of the world. The spiritual changes came later. They came, perhaps not unexpectedly, after starting to believe that a spiritual reality, whatever name one gives it, underpins all things. I will begin with the external events. Let Margaret first tell of the dream that led to our marriage.

Margaret and the dream

At the time of the dream I had just been going through another hard time in my life. Andy, my first husband, had died when he was only 51. We had been living in London and after his death I moved back to the family home in Breasclete on the Isle of Lewis. Instead of me buying another house somewhere in Scotland, my brother gave me the family house and croft. I was in the middle of renovating the house when I had the dream.

On the night of the dream I was really upset because of a disagreement with the builder. I was angry and sad with God and was saying to him 'Why me all the time, I seem to be the only one in the family who gets so much pain and sorrow?'

I fell asleep crying and woke up during the night. I dreamt that I was walking along a path and looked up and saw a gate in the distance with a man with his back to me standing at the gate. His hair was grey. There was no sign of a house or animals or anything around, just the man and the gate and a green field beyond. I slowly walked up to the gate and on hearing my footsteps, the person turned round. I recognised him to be Myles Campbell although I hadn't seen him for 31 years. I was very surprised. The black hair he once had was now grey. He recognised me immediately and said, 'Hello, how are you?' I said I was OK, but he seemed to understand that I was dreadfully unhappy.

He opened the gate and took my hand and invited me in to the field and we started walking. As we walked along I started telling him how I really felt, as I sensed him to be an understanding, kind and caring person. It was easy to tell him all about myself. We were walking along a path with green fields on both sides and it was all so peaceful. Then I woke up. Reality. I realised I was back in the real world. How I had wanted to stay in that peaceful place. I was so disappointed to wake up.

The dream was also a surprise because I hadn't been thinking of Myles in the intervening years since we met in 1964. Next day I was still thinking about the dream, but then I forgot about it and carried on with the renovation of the house. However, in the weeks and months and years ahead, that dream would come back to haunt me. Myles would come into my thoughts and I could see his face and the grey hair and the smile.

Although this was happening, I didn't tell anybody about it and I couldn't understand why it kept coming back to trouble me. It had never happened to me with any other dream before or since.

But this man, whom I hadn't seen for 31 years and of whose whereabouts and subsequent history I had no idea, became a distraction and worry for me. I was a Christian believer by then and I would pray for him even before I would pray for members of my own family, something that puzzled me greatly. I would burst into tears thinking of him. This continued for 3 or 4 years. Crazy? Yes, it was. I thought so too, and I just couldn't understand it. As a Christian, I didn't know what the dream meant. I had never heard of anything like it before, although I had heard many stories of people's experiences prior to and after conversion. I didn't think this dream had anything to do with the Lord being involved in any way. Perhaps I should have studied the Bible more closely where God frequently communicates with people through dreams, but that never occurred to me at the time. I never thought that I would be used in such a way. I had a rather low opinion of myself as a Christian, because I felt myself to be very imperfect in the Christian life and a poor example.

But before going on to tell the outcome of the dream I should go back and tell a little about my background and how eventually I became to believe in God and the Holy Spirit.

Early days – Breasclete and Inverness

I was born in Breasclete on the island of Lewis in a Gaelic-speaking family. My parents were both Christians and members of the Free Presbyterian Church. I was one of a family of nine and our upbringing was strict. It probably had to be to keep us out of mischief, as there was so many of us. Our home was filled with Christian love and security and although we didn't attend Sunday school, every Sunday was indeed a day of rest all that day. We went to church in the morning and evening and the afternoons were spent learning the Shorter and Mothers' Catechism. After supper we would learn and sing psalm tunes.

I remember a blackboard given to my parents by my uncle, who was a schoolteacher. The notes to the tunes were written on the board. We learned the tune first and then did Gaelic precenting. At family worship, we had to take turns precenting the psalms and then read a couple of verses each from the Bible, which was how we learned to read Gaelic.

The practice of precenting goes back to a time when people in church didn't have Gaelic Bibles and many couldn't read the language. The line was given out by the precentor and repeated by the congregation. Although the tunes, such as 'Kilmarnock' and 'Martrydom', have their roots in the English and Scottish Lowland musical tradition, in the Presbyterian churches in the Highlands they have a distinctive flavour of their own. There is freedom and ornamentation in the singing. For a Gaelic speaker there is no comparison between the psalms sung well in Gaelic and English psalm singing. A Gaelic congregation in full flow is an amazing spiritual experience. Why churches are abandoning such singing, where the people are still Gaelic-speaking, in favour of English singing is a real mystery.

At Communion times our house was always full of people and, despite there being eleven in our family, there were always beds made available for church members who stayed for the weekend from other parts of the island.

Preparing for the Communions, which happened only twice a year, was a busy time. All the rooms had to be immaculate and the silver polished, and also the tablecloths starched! The baking proceeded with the making of cakes, scones and pancakes and black and white and fruit puddings. There was also fresh wild salmon. During the weekend the kitchen was a hive of activity, everything supervised by mother. We were taught from a very young age to cook and help in all kinds of ways, and, indeed, it was an excellent learning experience for all of us.

I always wanted to be a nurse, so when I was accepted as a trainee nurse in a hospital in Inverness I was very pleased. I enjoyed the freedom of not having to go to church, or having to adhere to the rules we had to keep to at home. Training was very strict and some of the ward sisters were very particular about everything, and, of course, the Matron did a ward visit every day.

While I was training, I met Andrew and fell in love with him. Shortly after we met we had an argument and split up for a couple of months. During that period I met Myles and had a brief relationship with him. However, Andrew and I made up and we married when I finished my training. My mother was unable to attend our wedding in Inverness, because of family illness. On the day we were getting married, the family doctor, a Christian, visited my mother at her home in Lewis. He had a verse from the Bible for her – '... and he sent a man before them – Joseph, sold as a slave.'[1] She answered, 'Well, if that's the case, we know the Lord was with Joseph. Our daughter Peggy is getting married today.'

As it happened, this verse turned out to be of great relevance for me in future years. The story of Joseph became a key text for me.

When we first married we were able to buy a two-bedroom flat in MacDonald Street, Inverness, with a toilet out in the hall. The standard of living was certainly different to what I was used to in Lewis, but we coped well. While living there our son was born.

The week after our marriage, Andrew started work with MacGrouthers. They were wholesalers of meat and meat products, including lamb, beef, pork, pies and sausages. At first he was delivering meat to butchers in and around Inverness, but then decided to try the butchers and hotels on the Isle of Skye. He built up a very successful business there.

In 1968, tragedy struck our family. My brother, Alex Dan, who was only 11 years of age, drank the deadly weed-killer Parquet, thinking it was lemonade. This incident was not only devastating for the family but saddened the whole island. He was flown by air ambulance to Edinburgh Royal Infirmary, where an emergency lung transplant operation was performed, the first of its kind in Scotland, but, unfortunately, Alex Dan died three weeks later. I remember the funeral procession leaving the house, with Nicolson Institute pupils walking in front of the coffin and the mourners behind walking for about half a mile. Newspaper reporters from all over Scotland were there.

At that time, my son Ian was just two years. How I had to avoid the reporters! We all had to, they were everywhere. My parents' faith helped them through it all. I stayed with them in Breasclete for a few weeks afterwards and the little child in the house helped ease the situation a little.

In 1969 my daughter was born and, as we were rather crowded in the small flat, we got a council house in Inverness. This was a three-bedroom house with a back and front garden. What a delight that was. My father-in-law was a gardener, so with his help we had a lovely garden, front and back. I was so fortunate to have such nice parents-in-law. My mother-in-law was very fond of children, and she was also a very good friend.

We had many friends and family staying with us in the years we were living there. I enjoyed cooking and baking for them all and we always had a houseful at Christmas time.

About that time my husband decided to visit butchers on the Isle of Lewis to see if it was worthwhile for him to start up a run there for MacGrouthers. This worked out well as shops he visited were very interested. And just at that time my father had to give up the lorry he was driving, which meant he was without work. Fortunately, Andrew was able to give him a job. For my mother the verse the local doctor had given her when I married had come true when she saw the big van parked outside her door. Joseph had been sold into slavery but in the lean years he had been able to help his family far from Egypt.

We decided then to build a house in Breasclete as my uncle had assigned a croft to me. When the house was finished we moved to Lewis. I worked for a while in the Lewis Hospital; while I was working in the hospital, I started attending church. My father had died and that had affected me deeply.

During the months leading up to my father's death, I started getting palpitations at night and the fear of death was difficult to contend with. At that time I didn't believe in prayer or in God, but it was that experience which led me to accept that there is a God who is very near to us. I remember waking my son during the night; I was terrified and crying and saying to him, 'Ian, I'm going to die.' And he became so tired of this (he was in his early teens at the time). He would say, 'Oh, mum, not again.'

One day I was in the house all alone, just a couple of weeks after my father's death, and in the end I couldn't even lift a teacup with this fear of death. I was exhausted with crying and decided to sit down in the sitting-room to die. I found the Bible, opened it, and just as I thought I was definitely going to die, I read the words, 'Be still and know that I am God.'

As I was reading these words I felt something going through me from head to toe. I couldn't understand this, but the palpitations stopped and I immediately felt better. What did this mean? The following Sunday I thought I would go to church and so I prepared and took out the only hat I possessed, which was a straw one. We had a dog at that time and he got a hold of the hat and shot off outside with it. By the time I retrieved it, it was in bits and I couldn't go to church. Women attending the Free Presbyterian Church have to wear hats.

However, the following Thursday my mother asked me if I would take her to the Uig communion and I agreed. Rev. Alfred MacDonald was preaching and it was as if he had been following me with a notebook since I had the experience in the sitting room, and all the questions I had been asking myself since then he answered. I was amazed and greatly relieved. I understood that it was God who was striving with me all the time. Wow! I thought then that that was the end of all my problems, but in reality it was just the beginning.

• 2 •

My early days and my beliefs

While all this was happening to Margaret, I was living in Staffin, in the Isle of Skye. I moved there in 1992 after the break-up of my first marriage. Margaret was the last person in my thoughts. Yes, I had hazy recollections of a relationship with her and that she had left me, not I her, but such memories merged with the memories of numerous other relationships I had as a young man. I never expected to see or hear from her again.

By 1996 I was in a long term relationship with someone else and had built a house on my grandfather's croft. Staffin was where I was born, where my mother was from and where I had been brought up for part of my childhood. I always had an affinity with the place and looked on it as my spiritual home. Little did I know at the time how much of a spiritual home it would become and what would happen to me in the next twelve years. If someone had told me what would happen, I wouldn't have believed them.

But in order to tell where I was spiritually at the time Margaret was having her dream, it is necessary for me to tell the story of my childhood and how my beliefs developed throughout my life up to the time of meeting Margaret. The stages were childhood, agnosticism and a belief in naturalism, doubts about naturalism, appreciating the world as 'miracle', and acknowledging the supernatural element in experience.

Childhood

My father had been a lay preacher with the Free Church of Scotland, or missionary as they called them. For many, a 'missionary' sounds like someone who goes abroad to other countries, but there were 'home missionaries' who never left Scotland and he was one of these. Missionaries weren't qualified as ministers but performed the same tasks, apart from officiating at weddings, baptisms and funerals, and for much less pay. They would spend a few years in a place and then be moved on by the Church to somewhere else. That is why I was in Staffin between the ages of 8 and 12.

I attended church twice on the Sabbath, plus Sunday School and a prayer meeting on Wednesday. There was also family worship in the morning and at night. The Bible was looked on as the inspired word of God.

This upbringing had a profound effect on me. From a very early age I was sensitive to what was being claimed for the Bible. Namely, that God was in Christ reconciling the world to himself, that he sent his Son to die for the sins of mankind, that he rose from the dead on the third day and that he called certain people to follow him and that he gave those people eternal life if they believed in him.

Even as a child, my first reaction was to rebel and to shelve the issue. It could wait till later when I would know more. I clearly remember saying this to myself when I was five years old.

Later as a 10–12 year old I began to have more serious doubts. My parents bought a children's encyclopaedia from a travelling bookseller. I devoured it. It was, of course, written from a contemporary Anglo-centric secular point of view – this was in the 1950s. This also had a profound effect on me. At an early age I was confronted with two conflicting world views, both alleging to be the one true version of existence. What was given in the encyclopaedia was presented as mere factual truth. This was the latest in human knowledge and the tone of voice implied that it would be silly for anyone to contradict what was the product of the latest scholarship and scientific research. I had come up against the autocratic world of imperialist knowledge – as I found out later, a peculiarly prejudiced and partial view of the world. The preaching of the church had the same air of certainty about it. What was one supposed to believe?

One of the sections in the encyclopaedia dealt with the theory of evolution. This to me, at that age, seemed to be in complete contradiction to the creation story in the Bible. One was a naturalistic story which told of a natural and non-vitalist emergence of life. The other gave a supernatural explanation. At that age I had no experience of supernatural events. Stories, yes, but these were just stories and couldn't be proved in any way. The naturalistic record of events began to sound more plausible to me by the day and I began to find all kinds of reasons for not believing the Bible.

Agnosticism and naturalism

Thus at an early age I became an agnostic and rationalist. Apart from my belief in science and naturalistic explanations, I found many other ways to contradict the Bible and to excuse myself from believing. If he was such a merciful God, why did he create a world where there was so much suffering and why in a world where suffering was a possibility, no, a certainty, why did he not prevent suffering? Why was salvation limited to an Elect? If Christianity alone was true, what would happen to those millions of Indians and Chinese who happened to have a different religion?

It was going to be a long time before I would discover my errors, or rather, as I look on it now, before the transcendent reality we call God would show me the error of my ways. At that time and for many years afterwards I was in a place of despair. I would have liked to believe what my parents told me, but I found it impossible, and I had no faith to put in its place. If I had any explanations, they were materialistic. I distinctly remember at the time touching objects, a wooden table for instance, and thinking how real it was and how everything had a cause and effect. What was real were the things one could see and touch. The rest was mere dreaming or wishful thinking.

As a teenager there was always the tension in me between the sensual and the spiritual, between love and lust. I was a sensual person and sensitive to the beauty of nature and women. I was determined to find out the real truth about life. Was there any purpose to it? Was there anything beyond what our senses could perceive or appreciate? Thus as a teenager I became a philosopher and poet. I was going to live according to what I believed. I certainly wasn't going to be a hypocrite, as I believed many in the church to be. How could they believe such rubbish, which seemed to contradict reason at every turn? Later, in my 20s, I would write a poem in Gaelic called 'Plannt Mara' which described my state of mind at the time:

Sea Plant

*I'm a sea plant / shaken from the shores of the world. / Perhaps
we'll meet / (there's a chance, / one among many) / in the middle of
the ocean, / that you were also / raised / in Calvin's earth, / the pre-
Copernican sky above you.*

*And that a day came / when the stars fell / and the sky broke in
bits, / and that you lost your land-made form, / floating / you and
I / forever more / on the cold empty seas / without root, without
guide.*[1]

Because morality was so strongly linked to the Bible and belief in God,
when I stopped believing in these – although I could never bring myself
completely to not believe in God – I also lost my moral bearings. I
reasoned that the only logical reason for morals was pragmatic and based
on self-interest and empathy for others. You could do whatever you liked
as long as you didn't hurt others, which conveniently left me plenty room
for a hedonistic lifestyle.

I said that I could never bring myself completely to not believe in God
and, looking back, it's interesting to note why this was so. I think it could
be traced to an instinctive and intuitive feeling that man – that conscious
being who could think about material things – could not have risen from
mere non-thinking matter. As if something that was merely material and
unconscious could over time acquire the ability to contemplate itself. As if
water could rise above the level to which gravity had taken it. It just didn't
sound right, that such a thing could happen.

It was much later, 30 to 40 years later, that science confirmed the
likelihood of a special Creation event through the discovery of the so-
called Big Bang theory of the origin of the universe. Before that it was
easy to believe that the universe was eternal, and if eternal there was
ample time for anything to exist and come to pass. In my imagination I
couldn't imagine something going out of existence, however hard I tried:
everything was energy and just changed to another form of energy. The
Big Bang theory and all that it implies changed all that.

The Big Bang event is **the** original miracle. My dictionary defines
a miracle as 'an event contrary to the laws of nature and attributed to

a supernatural cause.' Scientists cannot tell what there was before the Big Bang. The question doesn't even make sense, because time and the cosmos as we know it all came into existence at that millisecond. Before the existence of time there wasn't a 'before' and an 'after.' In that sense the origin event wasn't 'contrary to the laws of nature' because the laws originated with the event. But that makes it even more pertinent to ask why there were laws at all and where these laws came from, quite apart from the fine tuning of the cosmic constants that resulted in the kind of world we live in. The origin of the universe is a miracle of such stupendous proportions that it staggers belief. It is the creation from 'nothing' of an astounding plenitude regulated by cosmic laws of unimaginable finesse. It all points to a Creator of supreme power and intelligence.

It is important to grasp that the *evidence* for a Creation event from 'nothing' is as recent as the end of the 20th century, and that the philosophers of the Renaissance and European Enlightenment did not have access to this evidence, much less the philosophers of Greece. It puts some of the ideas of post-Enlightenment philosophers, such as Nietzsche, who talks of an eternal return, in perspective. For Nietzsche, or for anyone else, there will be no eternal return, or even a return, for the Cosmos is finite and of finite duration. No return unless, of course, the Supreme Power who is 'outside' the universe decrees otherwise. The Christian belief is that this Power has revealed itself to men and women in history and continues to do so. It is both outside the universe, in a form that can only be known through revelation, and inside the universe revealing itself in the creation itself and to the hearts of human beings.

As Bryan Magee observed, 'Nietzsche agreed with Schopenhauer that there is no God, and that we do not have immortal souls. He also agreed that this life of ours is a meaningless business of suffering and striving, driven along by an irrational force that we can call will.'[2] Nietzsche further believed that this world is all that there is. There is no transcendent reality. Therefore humans have to create their own values and values should be those which favour the strong, as happened naturally in the animal kingdom. 'The central values that we should embrace ... are those of life-assertion.'[3] No wonder the Nazis loved Nietzsche, although they totally misrepresented him. There was enough flawed philosophy there for them to hold on to and create havoc in the process. When man puts himself in the centre of the world and tries to create his own values, the inevitable happens: destruction and unhappiness follow. Whether the values are right wing or left wing, as in the revaluation of all values by Karl Marx, the ideals become distorted and twisted and end up in dictatorship, whether Communist, as in the Soviet Union, or Fascist, as in Germany and Italy.

This book is about miracle, the initial great miracle of the Creation and its evolution in time, but also the miracle in the lives of humans. For the miracle is occurring all the time in the lives and hearts of men and women, whether we realise it or not. The means used by God, the supreme witness, is the Logos, the Christ, the Word, God's rule and governor that became flesh in Jesus Christ.

But I am jumping ahead of myself with the story. In my younger days I didn't believe what I have just said. I continually argued that there couldn't be a merciful God. How could such a God create a world like ours where the law of the jungle reigned and one species survived by eating another? It was a jungle 'red in tooth and claw,' a case of dog eats dog. Even the so-called most advanced species, the human, survived by the same method. Life seemed to be a cycle of birth, suffering, sacrifice and death.

All my life I was dogged by these questions, exploring them mostly through poetry but also through philosophy. For many years I was stuck in the same place and there seemed to be no escape. I seemed to be a hopeless case as far as belief in the God of my parents was concerned. Reason would just not allow me to believe.

Little did I know that while I was struggling with philosophical questions and unbelief, God was preparing a way to enter my life in a manner that is quite beyond human agency to achieve. Quite extraordinary that God – the creator of the universe! – should bother to communicate with one of his puny creatures. It is unbelievable, yet I believe this has really happened. This book is the story of how the infinite communicated with the finite.

If the transcendent reality is *infinite,* then it will be present everywhere and at all times, and available to everyone. The God of eternity is also the God of time. Margaret and I are not claiming to be special in any way. Far from it. The testament of innumerable people through the ages attests to the presence of this infinite reality. Thousands, even millions, of people through the centuries have claimed that God has touched their lives. The question for the sceptic is how many people have to attest the presence of a supernatural being operating in their lives before it becomes a true fact? The evidence of two people is enough to convict a person in a court of law. When does the evidence become sufficient for the sceptic?

· 3 ·

Margaret's life in Benbecula

The house was renovated but I was still only 50 and I needed more in my life than living in the family home, however beautiful. I needed a job and jobs were few and far between in Lewis. A post was advertised in the Stornoway Gazette for a nurse with the Ministry of Defence in Benbecula. I wasn't enthusiastic about going to work in Benbecula, so far from home, and in fact had thrown my copy of the Gazette, in which I had seen the advert, in the bin. Later in the week one of my brothers mentioned to me that he had seen the advertisement in the paper and that it might be a suitable job for me. It made me think again and I applied for the job, although the deadline for applications was past. I was given an interview, and landed the job. I was, in fact, the only applicant.

I enjoyed working in Benbecula and made many friends. One good friend in particular, Sylvia, was my prayer partner. When we came to know each other well, we would meet in my house most days for a cup of tea, and prayer of course. About a year after being in Benbecula, I was at an Easter convention and met a man in whom I felt I could confide my concerns about the dream. I hadn't told anybody up till then, but I felt I had to tell somebody. He was a missionary and teacher in the Yemen and was from the Isle of Lewis.

He said that he had had a similar experience before he met his wife and that he believed the dream he had was from God and that my dream was also from God. God knew all about Myles and I should pray for him, he said. I was greatly relieved that the one and only person I had confided in understood what I had told him and did not make fun of it, and had a similar experience himself. From then on it was easier for me to tell my close friends about the dream.

The worry concerning the dream continues

After about a year in the job one of my duties was to go to the remote island of St Kilda one week in seven as nurse for the maintenance staff in the Army base and visitors to the island. It is an awesome island of great natural grandeur. For me, it was a place where I felt particularly close to God. But even there the memory of the dream pursued and bothered me.

One day Sylvia mentioned that she was going to a Christian gathering called *Skye Live* on the Isle of Skye. This didn't mean much to me at the time but in the days that followed I felt that I should go with her, and on the following Sunday at the church service, I asked if I could join her in Skye. She was delighted. It would be a new experience for me, as I had never been to a Pentecostal event. We both had a wonderful time and we went back to Benbecula invigorated.

Life continued, and so did the concern about the dream.

I told a friend about the dream and it turned out that Myles had been her teacher in school on the Isle of Mull, but she didn't know where he was then. She phoned her mother that evening and learned that he was living either in Skye or Inverness. The next person to whom I mentioned the dream was a teacher and she had a daughter who taught in Portree. She phoned her daughter who told her that Myles was teaching in Portree. Now I knew that he was in Skye.

A year passed and it was time for *Skye Live* again and Sylvia and I were going. The day before we were due to leave, I had an awful day thinking about Myles and the dream. I was in tears. He was a greater worry than ever. When Sylvia came in, as usual, in the afternoon, she felt I should contact him. I didn't agree with her, although I knew he was living on Skye. I wasn't at all sure about phoning. It was as if I was phoning a stranger. Such a ridiculous thing to do! What would the man think if I told him I had a dream about him?

But I wanted rid of my concern with the dream and the only way I knew of doing so was to meet him and tell him about it. By meeting him and telling him I hoped that I would no longer have the albatross of the dream. Sylvia and I agreed that she should phone two friends and that if she got Myles's address and telephone in two calls and I phoned the number once only and he answered the phone himself then the Lord was in the middle of what we were doing. And so it happened. With her second call she got his details and with my first call he answered the phone. We were all set for *Skye Live* and I would meet him there, or so I hoped.

• 4 •

Nothing but silence

In my twenties I worked in the Prison Service in Inverness and then Perth. From Perth I went to Edinburgh and worked as a wages clerk with Edinburgh City Council for a couple of years before going to Edinburgh University, where I did Gaelic, English and History. Afterwards I did my teacher training in Jordanhill College, Glasgow and ended up in the Isle of Mull as a Gaelic teacher. From the time I was at Edinburgh University I wrote my poetry in Gaelic, what was for me the language of the heart. Here is a translation of 'Gealach Shàmhach' (*Silent Moon*) written when I was in Mull:

> *We / in the wood. / Above it the sun, / above it the moon. / Moon world, / sun world, the one burning, / the one wan. / The moon is pale / in the same sky /in which the leaves are falling. / If I should catch the pale moon / the sun would fall / if I should catch the leaf.*

> *Mud smell / in the brown path, / the leaf falling / according to nature's laws, / and dying. / It will fall forever, / dispersing, / uniting.*

> *The pale leaf / in the mud, / the white swan on the wave / and the sun without light.*

> *What town is this / that is so silent? / For God's sake / say something / about unity, about scattering.*

> *The leaf broke in a thousand pieces. / The moon was silent.*[1]

The moon represents the spiritual dimension of experience, while the sun symbolises the rational. This really is a bleak poem representing a bleak and hopeless state of mind. The 'moon' world, that part of our experience as human beings that could potentially communicate with us and tell us that there is something beyond mere decay, is absolutely silent. Instead time, with its cycle of birth and dissolution reigns supreme. This is a poem of despair, of dreadful absolute despair.

A poem written when I was 40 years of age called 'Sùil air Ais' (*Looking Back*) paints a similar picture. It indicates quite clearly how I felt about matters of the spirit at the time:

Forty and still blind / without an answer (and I never will have) / for the universal questions / – despite these being all there is, / although we often deceive ourselves / when we see a day like today / fresh, bright, and the sun gilding the earth, / grass, street and bay. I'd wish then there weren't such questions, / as the question of death, truth, / or what Love, God, Christ means, / and a thousand other things undisclosed, / until my brain is a whirlpool – / but I return, and return again / in my shell of a boat.

I thought once there was an answer, / that fruit would fall from the tree of knowledge / and that I'd eat the apple of wisdom, or that a voice would speak / with undeniable authority / from the pillar of fire. Nothing but silence. / Nothing but miracle after miracle / as anybody must confess / who considers Nature or one atom / of the world's material, but all natural, reasonable, / to an extent. What I wanted was a trumpet, a fire, / which would prove there was something intelligent / beyond the veil. / The world / or God (whatever kind of being it is) / doesn't work like that. Nothing but silence – / and a feeling that cannot be expressed / that there are things that want to speak, / and that do, and do not quite reach us / because they don't speak our language.

They will come one day, perhaps, pouring / out of some sky. / But before that happens perhaps we won't care / not care at all.[2]

That is exactly how it was. Nothing but silence. I was exactly in that place because I couldn't see beyond naturalism and materialism. Certainly, the miracle and beauty of nature spoke to one's heart and mind, but there was a huge gap between that and human speech; between the vague, though beautiful, messages of Nature and the propositional utterances of human beings. Yes, Christians and other religions claimed that the divine spoke in scripture through the voices of God's messengers. But then, the voices seemed to contradict themselves and, therefore, who, or what, was one to believe?

This was my dilemma and the dilemma of my contemporaries. There is an increasing gap between mainstream secular opinion and what orthodox churches believe about God and the Bible. For many in the modern world, the word 'God' is a word with no content. No one better analysed the situation in the 20th century than Francis A. Schaeffer.

Schaeffer makes a distinction between the 'upper storey' and the 'lower storey.' In the upper storey go things like God, Grace and universals. In the lower storey are Nature and particulars. Nature and the study of nature since Thomas Aquinas's time became more and more important; they became in fact autonomous and began to push out the need for an upper storey, the need for God. This paved the way for an 'autonomous Humanism.'

For scientists who are opposed to a supernatural explanation, science no longer has to take God or the supernatural into account and 'the uniformity of natural causes in a closed system has become the dominant philosophy among scientists.'[3]

Truth itself becomes relative and man becomes the centre of the universe. The upper storey now has 'faith' and the lower storey 'rationality', but reason cannot now connect one to what is in the upper storey. Schaeffer calls this the 'line of despair.' God no longer reveals Himself in propositional language in the Bible and so we arrive at Kierkegaard (1813–1835) and the idea of the leap of faith, a non-rational leap of faith. There can be no longer any connection between the upper storey of faith and the lower storey of reason.

Life seen through the lens of reason is meaningless and man's reason cannot connect with whatever is in the upper storey. And so man tries to make the leap to meaning by whatever means he can. The New Theology, for example, uses non-rational connotation words, such as 'resurrection', 'crucifixion', 'Christ' and 'Jesus.' For the New Theology these are merely connotation words and only give 'an illusion of communication.' This 'Christ' and 'Jesus' is not God revealing himself in a specific historical event and an actual resurrection. They are only emotively charged words to which people can respond. 'Being separated from history and the cosmos, they are divorced from possible verification by reason downstairs, and there is no certainty that there is anything upstairs.'[4]

Secular existentialist philosophers and thinkers try to find meaning in a meaningless world by different means whether it's Jean-Paul Sartre (who thought that, looked at rationally, the universe was absurd) with his idea that the human being has to authenticate himself by an act of will. It doesn't really matter what you do as long as you decide to do something![5] Or there's Jaspers idea of having a 'final experience' which comes from the upper storey. You cannot order it, it just comes, or it might never come. Others like Aldous Huxley talks about 'first order experience' which is an experience of the upper storey. In order to have this kind of experience, Huxley advocated the use of drugs.

Schaeffer's answer to all the doubts of secular philosophers and liberal theologians was to write a book with the title *The God Who is There*. His answer to a meaningless world in a naturalistic universe where man is created by a process of chance in a world of time is to believe in a creator God who revealed himself to man in the Bible. In other words Schaeffer goes back to historical creedal Christianity.

I was very much in the condition described by Schaeffer into my fifties. My problem was that having read the philosophers, and even some liberal theologians, I realised that my problem was also theirs. I am telling this in order to make clear how profound my problem was. It was not just my problem; it was the problem of critical thinking everywhere. Don Cupitt, who authored a controversial BBC television series entitled *The Sea of Faith* in the 1980s and wrote a book of the same name, is very explicit about the nature of the new theology.

He claims, for instance, that 'all vital modern religious thought since Kant has been (unconsciously, more often than consciously) creative, expressive and non-realist.'[6] The important point to emerge from Kant's analysis according to Cupitt is 'that the power that orders the world and turns chaos into cosmos is no longer ascribed to an objective metaphysical Creator, but simply to the human mind.'[7] The Gospels also are now seen as 'entirely human.' For Cupitt, God is simply 'the sum of our values, representing to us their ideal unity, their claims upon us and their creative power.'[8]

For Cupitt and theologians of like persuasion, there is no-one objective to pray to any more. God is only a word for the human being's ideal values. Similarly for Paul Tillich. At Santa Barbara, shortly before he died, Tillich was asked if he prayed and he replied, 'No, but I meditate.'[9]

At the beginning of the 21st century such secular humanism is common throughout society. It started with philosophy, with Kant, Hegel and Kierkegaard, and in the 20th century permeated the arts, general culture and finally theology. It means people find it difficult to believe in a God who is real and who can answer prayer. There is a decline in church attendance, not because people don't have a need for Transcendence, but because they cannot connect with the kind of Transcendence on offer. There are people who can accept traditional religion without questioning or thinking too much about it. Others go to church from habit. They are the kind of people who Kierkegaard would consider dead to the true inner life, for they are not striving for a true inner faith.

I didn't go to church for years because the services seemed irrelevant. Ministers just did not talk about the real doubts I, and, I assume, others had about the nature of reality, including the nature and existence of God. This to me is where churches are failing. They have to address the real doubts and questions people have. They just can't be swept under the carpet.

Before I came to believe in a God who answers prayer and who is more real than anything, I was full of these very doubts. They are all too evident in my poetry. Here are some translated examples from *A' Gabhail Ris* (Accepting), published when I was 50:

New Skin

This reality surrounds me / like a body, a head, / a new pervasive skin – an invisible sleet / soaking me to the core. When the trembling starts / this covering will be useless, / and there is no / god-created material / to make another.[10]

I was talking of the post-modern world and how I was locked into the belief system of the philosophers mentioned above. There seemed to be no escape. In another poem I say:

We are like dreams which last / a year or two – dreams / dreaming dreams. / What will / assuage the fiery world or the spark? / Language of us, of our brain, / a part, we of language. / We are flames in a fire, / lighting us and burnt in it.[11]

And from the same series of poems:

The Kaleidoscope

I placed my eye to the lens / to watch the multi-coloured patterns, / a wonderful world created / and disappearing almost before it is visible.

The colours perfectly ordered, / splendid in organised joy, / like the chill stars in the sky / strangers to a single feeling.

With a slight movement of the hand / I create new worlds: / the scales fall like a shadow, / I recognise that everything is in my vision –

lights forming a pattern, / the mind giving them its own slant, / nothing there but a pattern in the eye / and patterns dissolving uselessly.

emptiness in mobile colours, / as MacLean once perceived / as he noticed a heron / seeking food as a human does;

alive for a moment in the light / as a precious or empty pattern, / entering the cold deplorable grave, / going eternally from sight.[12]

I have translated enough of my poetry to show the awful place I was in. 'New Skin' and 'The Kaleidoscope' were written in the early 90s. As indicated earlier, it is a place of despair, and there appears to be no means of escape. In the late 90s my views began to change. In a poetry collection *Saoghal Ùr* (New World) published in 2003, my belief in a Transcendent reality and my struggle to come to terms with this are evident.

'The Soul of Truth'

In 1996–98, while Margaret was in Lewis and later in Benbecula, quite unaware of what I was up to, and contending with the dream she had in the autumn of '95, and which troubled her so much, I was struggling with trying to formulate what my own philosophical position was as regards the problems identified by writers like Francis Schaeffer, Don Cupitt and others. I was doing this because events which had happened to me since coming to Skye from Mull, and previously, had convinced me that naturalistic explanations were inadequate.

The titles of notes I was writing at the time will give a taste of what I was working on at the time. Here is just a small sample: 'The possibility of absolute moral values', 'Bottom up or top down', 'The four modes of apprehension: thought, feeling, sensation and intuition', 'Christianity versus nihilism', 'The universe as divine mirror', 'The destructive aspect of the divine', 'Achieving a truthful point of view', 'The eternal identity of the human being', 'Whole-forming – overview', 'The hidden Christ', 'The opposites in the light of the unconditioned.'

On 3rd January 1998 I wrote about 'The Soul of Truth – reasoning and intuition.' It is evident that I was struggling to see a unity behind appearances. I was moving towards a holistic view of things. I was trying to unite the material world with the world of value and I found it hard. There are in the universe 'souls of truth,' I wrote. 'They are the truth-seeking souls and they look on life as a journey towards truth ... *The end truth is an experiential truth.*'

I was beginning to distrust reason and to set more store on intuition. I was becoming convinced of 'the unity of all things' and to believe in "a whole-making 'force' which works through and in all things."

It is clear from these notes that I was less sceptical by then than I was when I wrote the earlier poetry. Quite apart from the intuitions I had that there was 'a superintending Wisdom permeating all things,' there were other reasons why I was changing my mind from an attitude of agnosticism to an attitude of disbelief in naturalism. They were discoveries in cosmology and science and, linked to the latter, the realisation that the world is pure miracle, and synchronistic and supernatural events in my own experience. Thus even before Margaret came into my life for a second time, my world view was changing.

• 5 •

An unexpected phone call

So it was that in the 90s, before I met Margaret again after nearly forty years, the silence to which I referred in the poem 'Sùil air Ais' (*Looking Back*) was to some extent broken. It wasn't that a voice spoke 'with undeniable authority / from the pillar of fire', but there was a voice and, although it was soft, it was persistent. Synchronistic events, the feeling of the unity of all things, the sense of the numinous and of the miraculous, the belief in a creation event, the findings of science, of which I will have more to say later, all led me to a growing belief in a transcendent reality behind appearances.

It was as if I was being prepared for the events which were going to happen. For although I believed in God and in his Son, Jesus Christ, they weren't as real for me as they would become. It is one thing to believe in God in a kind of theoretical way as a result of the various types of experience that I've mentioned. There is of course nothing wrong with that, and it gives one a good feeling. But it is quite another thing to come to believe, because of specific things that happen to you, that the transcendent reality, God, the Supreme, the Lord – call it what you like – is dealing personally with you as an individual. Could the person, me, the agnostic sceptical me ever come to such a belief? The poetry I wrote is evidence of how sceptical I was. How could such a person ever believe? God speaking to a person through dreams and through events? Don't be silly! That just doesn't happen nowadays. Perhaps it happened in Biblical times when people were naive and of a different mindset, but not now, not in the 21st century.

Then one day as I sat in the living room in Staffin in the summer of 2000 the phone rang. Much to my surprise it was someone who I had not seen or heard of for 36 years. The conversation went something like this:

ME: Hello.

MARGARET: Hello, this is Margaret Goodall, do you remember me?

ME: (pause, and great surprise) Er ... yes ...

MARGARET: Well, I've got something to tell you, but I'd rather not tell you over the phone. I'd like to meet you and tell you. I'm a Christian now and I'm going to *Skye Live* tomorrow, would you like to meet me at the tent in Broadford?

I was, to say the least, stunned by this invitation and not a little puzzled. Why was this woman phoning me? Was she trying to save my soul? That was the first thought that came to me. And if so why? After all it was 36 years since we had last seen each other and it was her who had jilted me; or at least left me for someone else.

I half-promised to meet her at the tent, just to get rid of her. When tomorrow evening came, I decided not to go. The more I thought about it, the more convinced I was that she was in evangelical mood and for some reason best known to herself that she had picked on me. I wasn't to be taken in. Meantime, God, the transcendent, call it what you will, through Margaret was not going to let go of me that easily. Here she continues the story.

Margaret tells of *Skye Live* and the sequel

Skye Live was in its 2nd year. It was a Christian charismatic weekend event with invited speakers, among them the Rev. Ian MacAskill, a Free Church minister from Uist whose services I attended in Benbecula. Part of the ministry was healing and being touched by the Holy Spirit. A marquee tent was set up in the car park opposite the Church of Scotland in Broadford and although not full, the event was well-attended.

It was there I waited at the door for Myles to come. I asked an elder if he knew him and would he recognise him. O yes, he knew him all right, but I would be better not knowing him. 'He's not your type', he said. Later, one or two others who had read his poetry warned me to steer clear of him. It looked as if I wouldn't need to. There was no sign of Myles inside or outside the tent. Once I had stood him up, now he had done the same to me.

When the service began, I went in and sat beside Sylvia. The Rev. MacAskill officiated. His text was Matthew 5:15 'Neither do men light a lamp, and put it under a bowl. Instead they put it on its stand, and it gives light to everyone in the house.' And he said the theme of his address would be 'Go Johnnie, go!' We started listening to the service. I had given up on Myles. It was obviously not meant to happen and we weren't going to meet.

During the service Sylvia nudged me and said, 'I think the Lord wants you to phone him.' I shook my head and said, 'No way!' As the service continued I got the next nudge and she said, 'I feel sure you have to call him.' As she said the words Ian MacAskill said, 'If you have had an experience with the Lord, you mustn't hide it under a bushel. But you must tell others, so go Johnnie go, and go, Margaret, go!' When he said these words I felt something going through me and knew his words were for me. I would have to obey. When I told Ian MacAskill afterwards that he had said these words, he couldn't remember saying them. But he did say them, for his sermon was taped, and I have the evidence on tape. He didn't know at the time about the dream.

When we got back to the B & B, I phoned Myles again and we arranged to meet the following day in a cafe in Portree. He thought there was no harm in meeting and discussing whatever was causing me the problem. I assured him that I wasn't trying to convert him, something that wasn't in my power. In the morning after the service I went forward for prayer and explained briefly the dream and that I was meeting the person in the dream. Although I didn't give the name of the person. Would they pray for me? Was I doing the right thing? The late Rev. Jack Macarthur prayed and assured me that I was on a mission for the Lord. Joe Ewing, who was one of the speakers at the event and who is known for his prophetic gift also prayed. He asked me what this 'miles' he was getting was, could I explain it. I said, 'Yes, his name is Myles.'

'Well, he said, this Myles is going to travel thousands of miles for the Lord, but he must first put his heart knowledge where his head knowledge is.' And he wished me a good journey and said that the Lord was with me.

I set off for Portree and waited in the cafe for Myles. When he came I recognised him from the dream. He had aged, as I had, and had grey hair as in the dream. We chatted and I told him about the dream and that I had been concerned about it for the past four years. I had wanted to meet him to tell him, in the hope that once I had told him that would be the end of the matter. 'It's over to you now,' I had said. I had washed my hands of the whole thing.

He was quite moved by the story and impressed that anyone should be praying for him. He appeared to me to be quite sad and after we parted I felt so sorry for him that I sat in the car and cried, not knowing why. It didn't make any sense to me. We had said goodbye and never expected to see each other again.

After *Skye Live* I was back in Benbecula and on my days off especially, much to my dismay, the Myles worry continued. I was haunted by this man. It was unreal, although it was easier to pray because I had seen and spoken to him and could put a face to the dream. After a few weeks I felt I had to go to Gairloch where Myles worked. I phoned him and he said he didn't see any harm in me coming to Gairloch if I wished.

On Sunday at coffee after the service I mentioned to a friend who knew the story that I had to go to Gairloch. She said she had just come back from there the day before and that she had a friend who did Bed & Breakfast. That was ideal for me and she even gave me her friend's address and telephone number. One other event – what Myles would have called a synchronistic one – happened on the following Tuesday. I began to doubt whether I was doing the right thing. I remembered that Myles stayed in the schoolhouse and that he cooked for himself. Wouldn't it be nice if I could get a piece of fresh salmon and salad and I could cook a meal for him? Within twenty minutes of thinking this, the phone rang and a friend who just had returned from Lewis with a fresh whole salmon offered me some as there was too much for them. I was surprised and delighted. It confirmed that I was doing the right thing after all!

In Gairloch I stayed at the B & B recommended by my friend, and Myles and I went for a meal together one night and on the other night we had a salmon salad in the schoolhouse. We talked about our past and got to know more about what had happened to us in the intervening years between our first meeting in Inverness and then. I had no idea where all this would lead but I thought meeting him this one more time and finding out more about him would finally put an end to the concern I felt for him. He told me he was in a relationship with someone else and that seemed to say all that needed to be said.

In any case, I wasn't there to start a relationship (I was very happy on my own and in a good job in Benbecula) but to get rid of this worry.

After my visit to Gairloch I went back to Benbecula and we didn't get in touch with each other again for about seven months. Myles lived his own life and I had no idea what was happening to him. By the end of the year, although I didn't know it, he had split up with his girlfriend. He was doing his own thing in Staffin and Gairloch and I was doing my own thing in Benbecula.

• 6 •

Doubts about naturalism – synchronicity

Jung and synchronicity

Margaret's life in Lewis and later in Benbecula was utterly different to mine. Her conversion meant that she had found God; or rather that he had found her. My life in the 80s and 90s in Mull and subsequently in Skye was one of philosophical speculation and poetic musing.

But despite all my lack of faith, and a lifestyle to go with it, I never stopped hoping to find out the real truth about life one day. For even in these days certain things which happened to me put doubts in my mind regarding naturalistic explanations. I had been reading C.G. Jung and learning about his notion of synchronicity, or meaningful coincidence. In his practice as a psychiatrist and in relation to his patients he had many synchronistic experiences. He had been treating a patient for depression and had not heard from the patient for some time, although he had arranged for him to get in touch if the person suffered a relapse. He was in a hotel room and suddenly awoke with the feeling that someone had entered the room. He was convinced that he had heard the door open. Then he remembered what he had felt as he wakened – 'a feeling of dull pain, as though someone had struck my forehead and then the back of my skull.'[1]

The following day Jung received a telegram. His patient had shot himself and 'the bullet had come to rest in the back wall of the skull.' For Jung this was a genuine synchronistic experience. It appeared that by 'a relativisation of time and space in the unconscious' he had been given information about something that happened elsewhere. He traces this knowledge to the 'collective unconscious.'

He notes that 'the unconscious had knowledge.' It is not clear how the unconscious can have knowledge, but it certainly appears to do so. The

Christian would say that it is God who has this knowledge. While Jung is quite sure that knowledge and meaning can come from the unconscious, the source of the meaning is indeterminate. Archetypes, 'whose content, if any, cannot be represented to the mind' are an intrinsic element in linking the physical world with the psychic. They are crucial in Jung's explanation of what could be the reason for sychronistic events.

In his introduction to Jung's work,[2] Anthony Storr explains what Jung meant by archetypes. They are not 'inborn ideas' but 'typical forms of behaviour which, once they become conscious, naturally present themselves as ideas and images.' Archetypes appear to be able to have a controlling power over 'ideas and images' although they are not conscious in themselves. The archetypes are felt as numinous. In other words, they are felt to have a great spiritual significance for the individual.

I find these ideas of Jung, particularly his talk of 'a reality outside space and time,' moving and extraordinary, because they link with so much of what I have experienced in my own life. I used to think of the world in naturalistic terms and as a closed system. But if what Jung is saying is true, and I now believe that it is, then, in my opinion, naturalistic explanations are not sufficient. We live in a world where the supernatural can intrude and can influence things in a major way. My own experiences, as described in this book, have convinced me that this is so.

The implications of a principle of synchronicity are stupendous. If there is such an acausal principle linking the mental world with the physical, it means that we live in a meaning-rich world, not in a meaningless one governed by blind laws of nature. Naturalism implies a world deprived of ultimate meaning because everything is derived from the natural workings of natural laws. The source of the laws is indeterminate. This in opposition to a universe linked intimately to an eternal realm and Source of which the universe is an expression.

What became clear to me, as I went through life, was the gulf between theoretical knowledge and personal experience. I had a lot of 'head knowledge' and believed Jung's personal testimony regarding synchronicity, but it was only when I had personal experience of what he was talking about that it really affected me. So it is with most things, theoretical knowledge or someone else's experiences are all very well, but it's only when they happen to yourself that they really hit home.

I didn't appreciate what Jung meant by synchronicity until I was in my thirties and even then I was not fully aware of the implications. Subsequent events, particularly what had happened in the last few years since meeting Margaret, have brought home to me with increasing force the implications of these occurrences. It is not one single occurrence but the accumulation of instances over many years that affects one. In the following pages I will be recalling synchronistic events which happened to me. It could be argued that some of them are just mere chance. Others are not so easily brushed aside.

But it is a long story. Certainly, it is the story of these events, but it is also the story of a convulsion in my world view. That convulsion did not come through wishful thinking. I can honestly say it was forced upon me. As I have already indicated, there are various strands to what precipitated this change in my *weltanschauung*: yes, personal events but also what science, particularly cosmology and microbiology, was discovering about our world.

Unusual events and synchronicities

The first unusual event happened to me when I was about 17 years of age. I was working as a deckhand aboard a cargo vessel, the Baron Inverclyde, and we were on the Tagus River in Portugal en route to West Hartlepool with a cargo of iron ore. We were anchored in the middle of the river. That morning, as I was walking nonchalantly along the alleyway in the crew's quarters a crew member, a man Scott from Glasgow, and his cabin suddenly impressed themselves on my mind for no apparent reason. It was like a flash of disquiet and it happened unasked and suddenly. I soon forgot about it. Until that evening.

We were lifting anchor and several deckhands – including me – were with the First Mate on the bow. It was getting dark and the Mate sent Scott and another hand to get a portable deck light in the nearest hold, where some were stored. In these ships the entrance to the hold was approximately 4' x 4' with a steel ladder going straight down. There was no light in the hold and Scott had lost his grip of the ladder and fell straight on to the iron ore. He was lacerated, bleeding and in a state of shock. We were anchored out from Lisbon and the medical services were radioed and a launch came out to our ship and took him to hospital. I left the ship after the voyage and never heard what happened to Scott, but I'm sure he recovered and would have been flown back to Glasgow.

It was afterwards I thought about the strange feeling I had had about Scott on the day of the accident. Of course, at that time I had not read Jung and had no idea of synchronicity. It was many years afterwards before I realised that it belonged to this category of events. I suppose I did puzzle over it and thought of it as a telepathic indication of what would happen in the future. But I had no idea of how this could be.

These events are one-off events and, therefore, are not susceptible to scientific verification, which demands that the scenario be repeated, and with scientific instruments present. This is hardly ever possible for events of this nature which happen to people without any warning. But enough people have experiences of this kind, however, as Jung asserted, to make them cry out for explanation. Too bad for science if some facts of existence are outwith its scope. Is it part of the fundamental constitution of the universe that science must be able to explain everything?

One other synchronistic event occurred to me in my teens when I was in the merchant navy. I had a dream of my sister-in-law in black as if she was in mourning. It was many years later that I discovered she had had a miscarriage around that time.

In my twenties, I experienced few meaningful coincidences of this kind. The surprise was that I had any at all. I was much more interested in having a good time, although I did continue to write verse and be interested in philosophical questions. I had stopped going to church for the reasons which I have spoken about earlier. In my late 20s one thing did happen which is perhaps worth recording, although it could be looked on as a mere coincidence. It did affect the course of my life.

I had recently moved to Edinburgh and was living in a bed-sit in Pilrig Street, while earning a living as a clerk with Edinburgh and District Council. It was a lonely existence, as I didn't know anyone in the city. I met the person who was to be my first wife at the Plaza Ballroom in Morningside. It no longer exists, but in the early 70s it was a popular place for young people. We dated once or twice, and then drifted apart. I wanted to ring her again but wasn't sure of her number.

About a week later I was in the bed-sit and wondering what entertainment the city had on offer. I looked in the Evening Times and noticed an advert for a casino near Tollcross. I had only been to a casino once before, but I was bored and I thought, why not give it a shot. As it happened, the casino was shut, but after leaving it who should I meet on the street but M. She had stopped to give directions to people and she shouted to me as I passed. We went for a coffee and started going out together and eventually married. I have always thought of that 'chance' meeting as a synchronistic event.

These events were a foreshadowing of what was to come. Stranger events than these were to 'invade' my life in the future, much stranger. Events which would contribute in a big way to the overthrow of my naturalistic world view. These happenings were, in a sense, a preamble to what was to come later.

I trained as a teacher, and eventually ended up on the Isle of Mull, because there happened to be a vacancy there for a Gaelic teacher. The translated poems I have already quoted 'Silent Moon' and 'The Kaleidoscope' show the frame of mind I was in at the time. This was despite having had some evidence from synchronistic events that things were not as I thought they were.

In Mull I did not usually go to church. But when I was alone one weekend, as M. was visiting her family in Edinburgh, that's where I ended up on Sunday morning. On the Saturday night when I went to bed the words, *I am the way, the truth and the life* came to my mind very strongly (John, 4, 6).

During the time I was in Mull, I had taken an interest in Japanese culture and in the religions of the East. Taoism itself, although not popular in Japan, talks of the Way, or the natural and spontaneous flow of the universe. The idea of the way or *do* is common in Japanese disciplines such as Chado – 'the way of tea', or the tea ceremony; Kodo – 'way of fragrance'; Jūdō – 'gentle way', one of the martial arts, and another martial art Kendo – 'way of the sword.' In contrast to the Eastern Tao or *do*, Christ's claim to be *the* Way came across to me particularly strongly, especially in contrast with the many ways to enlightenment to be found in Japanese religion and culture. Perhaps that is why that verse, which came to me before I slept, affected me so strongly.

In any case, I went to church, the Free Church, the following morning. I sat in the back seat, as far away from anyone's gaze as possible! You've guessed it, the verse the minister preached from was the verse that came to me so strongly before I slept. In church, I had opened the Bible at the psalms, it opened at psalm 25. The first psalm the minister chose was psalm 25. Of course, in the Free Church the psalms to be sung are not displayed on a board. Only the minister knows which psalm it's going to be. Coincidences, perhaps, but quite powerful for the person who experiences them.

In 1985, after having been a teacher for six years, I was given the chance to work as a Gaelic Development Officer with the Highlands and Islands Development Board in Inverness. It was something I wanted to try and I did a stint of 2 years with the Board before returning to Mull. For some time, I had had the idea of composing a poem about the road, or way. It was the way my mind seemed to work; an idea or image would be with me for weeks or months or even years and then one day the poem itself would come. I would write it down as it came to me, in an hour or two or even less, depending on the length of the poem.

I would drive home from Inverness to Mull every two or three weeks, usually stopping in Fort William for a bite to eat. This time I stopped at a local hotel and while waiting for my meal this poem about the road started to come to me and I quickly wrote what came to me. I couldn't finish it, and in any case my meal arrived. The poem was in Gaelic of course. Every poem I wrote was first written in my mother tongue. It is called 'A' Càradh an Rathaid' (*Mending the Road*). Here is how the poem starts:

With a yellow oilskin on / I mend the road / and fill the holes / with tar and gravel. / I remember the tar / how the bubbles would break / in the heat of youth. / Now / we mend the road / that goes nowhere.

A man came who said: / Put it there, my friend – / the road breaks beneath our feet. / The heart's tar hardens, / no sun to swell it. / It descends and climbs – / there is no ascent/salvation – / the only one for remedy.

37

A bird on the twig / singing by itself: / Little boy, little boy, / don't worry, / don't worry, / there is no road in the sky, / why do you mend / the road that goes nowhere?

The road is so devious, / mobile, tortuous, / hidden from view, / the endless vein-webs / in the body of creation, / one moment so whole / and the next in smithereens.[3]

It was unfinished and I had no idea how it would end. I sauntered along Fort William's main street. This wasn't my usual practice; usually I would have my meal and carry on to Mull. I was passing a pub and heard music and I went in. There was a bar at ground level and a few steps led up to the entrance to the second level. I had a half pint at the bar, took out what I had written and had a look at it. I would try and finish it later.

The music I had heard was dance music and it was coming from the upper level area. There were a couple of people at the entrance who appeared to be taking money for getting in. One of them was a bald-headed, middle-aged man. I noticed him because he seemed to be staring intently at me as I sat at the bar. I certainly had never seen the man before and had never been in that particular pub. I thought I would see what was happening in the upper area. I finished my drink and went to the door. He gestured for me to go in, no payment required.

There was another bar in the upper area and a band was playing in the corner. The place was practically empty. One or two were standing at the bar. After I had been there for a few minutes the bald man came in and chatted to the person next to me for a minute or so. I noticed that he spoke in a thick Lowland Scots accent, so thick that I could hardly make out what he was saying.

As he finished speaking to the other person, I said hello to him and asked what he did for a living. 'I work on the road near the King's House on the road to Glencoe', he said. What actually do you do? I asked him. He explained that he drove a lorry and supplied aggregate for the road-works. Our conversation lasted just a minute or two. He went back to the door and I went back to my half pint.

What had happened didn't immediately sink in. But as I stood at the bar it dawned on me that the ending of the poem had just presented itself to me in the shape of the old road mender. I left the pub after my half pint and carried on home. It was then that I wrote the ending to the poem, which goes:

Don't believe, don't believe
that it goes nowhere
(said the old man of the road);
everything will ripen
and the heart will be satisfied
with a symbol,
with the arteries' warm blood
and everything will arrive in its place
as in the beginning.

For now, fill the holes
and go forward:
everyone must travel/pass on –
and be mending.[4]

At the time, the poem seemed to be a good enough articulation of how I felt. As an expression of how I feel about the Way now, it is quite inadequate for it gives the impression that the heart can be 'satisfied with symbols.' Now I realise that symbols, however powerful they may be in the arts, including poetry, are not meaningful in a precise enough way. This book is about the finding of such meaning, and this 'meaningful coincidence' which happened to me in Fort William in 1985 was a small step on the way. Although symbols are not precise, the actual meeting of the poem with the road mender was extremely precise.

Since then I have often thought about what happened and the sequence of events leading up to the completion of the poem. I find naturalistic explanations quite inadequate. The congruence of the mental and physical events is quite inexplicable. The first part of the poem, written in the hotel is about the meaninglessness of existence. 'There is no ascent' could be translated 'there is no salvation.' The road the bird describes is a 'road in the sky', in other words, a non-existent road that is going nowhere. Verse four laments the ephemerality of all things, 'one moment whole / in the next crushed.'

The fact that I then met a man who was mending the road gave an unexpected meaning to the road and thus to life. The events and the way they happened gave a promise of meaning in existence. Looking back, to me the chances of all this happening by chance are virtually nil. Was life, or even Transcendence, trying to tell me something? Whether they were or not, I was obviously still not prepared to be convinced of the meaningfulness of life, as the poems from *A' Càradh an Rathaid* (1994), quoted earlier (but written years after this experience), 'New Skin' and 'The Kaleidoscope', illustrate.

There is one other example of synchronicity which happened before Margaret and I married which is worth telling. I was dating someone and, for reasons that are not necessary to go into, I didn't trust her. One morning I tried to explain to her how important trust was in a relationship. I said to her: 'It's like an electric kettle and you switch it on and it works. Perhaps it works several times in a row, and then it won't work. Again it works several times, and then it won't work. It's like a relationship', I said, 'things go well for several weeks and then the relationship breaks down because one person does something they promised not to do. The other person forgives, but then the same thing happens again, and again. That I said is precisely like a kettle that sometimes works and other times won't work.' R. just sat and listened.

I went through to the kitchen to make myself a coffee. You've guessed it, the kettle wouldn't work. The kettle was quite new, a few months old at the most and the switch had worked perfectly up to then. Now, when I tried to switch the kettle on, it would sometimes work and other times it wouldn't. The kettle was thrown out, and not long afterwards our relationship came to an end. I'm well aware that kettle switches can become faulty, but that it became faulty just after talking about it that morning, *in the context that we did*, is the point.

A reality 'outside' of time and space

The accumulation of synchronistic events of this kind continues in my life up to the present day. They appear to confirm Jung's view that 'the psychic lies embedded in something that appears to be of a non-psychic nature.' To again quote what Dr Anthony Storr says in his introduction to his *Jung, Selected Writings*: 'Jung came to think of archetypes as existing in this reality outside space and time, but manifesting themselves in the individual psyche as organizers ... One reason why Jung thought of archetypes as existing outside space and time was that he believed them responsible for what he called 'meaningful coincidences ...'[5]

It is a striking phrase – 'this reality outside space and time.' Since Kant's time it has been difficult to think of a reality outside of space and time. For Kant space and time are subjective forms of human sensibility. He inaugurated the 'Copernican' revolution in philosophy and this involves a totally new way of looking at the way we acquire knowledge, 'instead of thinking of our knowledge as conforming to a realm of objects, we think of objects as conforming to our ways of knowing.'[6] Because objects come to us through 'forms of sensibility' and pure concepts and categories through which they are thought, we can never know them as 'they may be in themselves.'[7] Kant sees human knowledge as 'limited to appearances or phenomena, whereas things-in-themselves or noumena are thinkable but not actually knowable.'[8] One of the consequences of the limitation thus set on human knowledge is '... to rule out virtually all traditional metaphysics.' This means that 'transcendent' questions such as the 'existence of God' cannot be answered by 'an appeal to possible experience.'[9]

However, this does not mean that Kant demolished the possibility of belief in God. What he claimed was that the existence of God could not be proved or disproved by reason. He had other reasons for believing in God. As Hans Küng says:

> This is the very thing that must not be misunderstood. Kant's view is often said to be that there cannot be any experience of God, since the latter is a pure concept of reason, a regulative principle, to which there can be no corresponding experience. But, as against this, according to Kant, 'an experience of God is possible, not in the sense that experience would make known to me the God whom I could not know without it, but in the sense that I can experience God if I already know him.' This is not a vicious circle, for – as we learnt – according to Kant, God's existence is already certain from another source.[10]

So Kant does not look 'beyond' to a 'transcendent' but rather within 'to the preliminary condition of possibility.' 'God ... is the condition of the possibility of morality and happiness.'[11] And we could add, just as the condition of the possibility of a cosmos, of an intelligible world, will be the laws which allow a cosmos to come into being. The laws are not a product of our minds nor of the material of which the world is composed; rather, they govern the material to make it a cosmos, a world which makes sense. We may not be able to prove this by logic but deep intuition, deeper than reason, tells us this must be so.

The importance of Jung's acausal principle can be seen in the light of Kant's idea of how the possibility of knowledge of the transcendent is curtailed. That is, the knowledge is not obtainable from sensible data or from reason. Meaningful coincidences don't contravene reason and neither do they derive their meaning from something which is non-sensible. Rather they happen in the normal course of events but are pregnant with meaning. They *could* be a means used by a transcendent reality to convey meaning in the 'natural' world without contravening the laws of nature. Information is given without breaking what science likes to look at as a closed system of natural laws. From my own experience, I am convinced this is the case.

I have already said that these coincidences which personally happened to me started doubts in me concerning the truth of naturalism and materialism. But I still didn't know what these coincidences meant. Why did at least some of them appear to be meaningful? For a long time I was concerned with the disparateness and apparent disunity of all things. In one poem, 'To Truth – what else?' I say:

Everything froth / on a raging sea / going out of sight.[12]

and the poem ends

The one behind the dream? / I've no idea. / The veil trembles.[13]

Blind chance or a self-organising universe

The search to find that unity through reason failed. For wherever reason looked, it only found death, dissolution, decay. It found only the 'arrow of time', a subject dealt with in a book of that name by Dr Peter Coveney and Dr Roger Highfield. For them this irreversibility of time is 'unavoidably linked' to 'the birth of time and of the universe itself.' 'The birth of time ... becomes an inevitably one-way process. It is the ultimate manifestation of time's arrow.'[14]

There was on the one hand this 'arrow of time', cosmic and universal in its operation, from the great galactic wall to molecular level. Nothing, it seems, can escape the juggernaut of time and the processes of dissolution. When death comes to the individual, there is no going back. It seemed to me and to sweet reason as if this was an absolute and that talk of 'eternal life' was wishful thinking.

But despite the seeming impregnability of the 'arrow of time' and its apparent absoluteness, there are, in opposition to reductionism, other ways, and others after that, of looking reality in the face, and coming back with a quite different story. One important way is the intuitive path to truth. It is the holistic way in contrast to the reductive way. It is the soaking in of the million things and intuitively sensing what it all means.

Even for the scientist, it is not fanciful to suppose that a more truthful view of what there really is can be obtained by holistic means than by a reductive methodology. Physicist Paul Davies writes: 'An increasing number of scientists and writers have come to realise that the ability of the physical world to organise itself constitutes a fundamental, and deeply mysterious, property of the universe. The fact that nature has creative power, and is able to produce a progressively richer variety of complex forms and structures, challenges the very foundation of contemporary science.'[15]

Davies says that the old atomistic view of the universe, going back to Democritus, is severely challenged by the new advances in physics, biology and other scientific disciplines. Where did the intricate order and organizing ability of the universe come from? We may indeed be witnessing a return to Aristotle's view of the cosmos. He regarded the universe 'as a sort of gigantic organism, unfurling in a systematic and supervised way towards its prescribed destiny.'[16] In today's language we might call this a cosmic blueprint, the unfolding of a plan which was there for all eternity.

Ilya Prigogine (1917–2003) was a chemist and Nobel Laureate whose work on dissipative structures and complex structures convinced him of the arrow of time and the unlikelihood of determinism. Rather matter appears to be creative and to have self-organising abilities. Davies quotes approvingly from Prigogine: 'We may one day perhaps understand the self-organising processes of a universe which is not determined by the blind selection of initial conditions, but has the potential of partial self-determination.'[17] And 'God is no more than an archivist unfolding an infinite sequence he had designed once and forever. He continues the labour of creation throughout time.'[18]

As a non-scientist, but as a person who is deeply interested in the discoveries of contemporary science, I never cease to be astonished at what modern science is uncovering. The role of intuition appears to me to be fundamental in the appreciation of the holistic and information-rich world of 'matter' of which we are part. Intuition questions how matter by itself could be so intelligent.

The unfolding of a cosmic plan and the self-organising abilities of matter speaks more for an idealist reality rather than a materialist one. That is, that the universe originated from an eternal and necessary mind rather than that mind is a by-product of contingent matter.

My first brush with the supernatural

Earlier, I spoke of synchronistic happenings in my life. Other events which happened to me could only be described as supernatural. As with synchronicity, the supernatural is significant for me as pointing to a numinous reality behind appearances.

In the old days in the Highlands of Scotland the supernatural was hardly considered such. The Gaelic scholar, Dr John MacInnes, while acknowledging the complexity of the issue, comments that 'what analysts call the supernatural or preternatural, or whatever, is in fact regarded by members of that society as part of the order of nature itself.'[1] Certainly, not so long ago in the Highlands of Scotland belief in second sight and *taibhsean* (ghostly apparitions of people), and even in fairies, was relatively commonplace. Few people would nowadays admit to a belief in fairies, but I do know people who firmly believe in *taibhsean* and other supernatural phenomena.

In my younger sceptical days I found it difficult to believe in so-called supernatural events. They belonged to an age of naivety and gullibility. I certainly wasn't going to be taken in by them! However, what happened to me and Margaret has forced me to reconsider.

It was on a summer's day in Staffin in 1994 or 1995 that I had the strangest experience of my life up to that point. I had had unusual experiences before that, some of which I have recounted. These come under the categories of the synchronistic or telepathic. This was different. It had the feeling of the weird or uncanny about it. It upset my expectation of the world as a predictable place. It overturned the calculations I had of the world as rational and reasonable – the Humean expectation that cause follows effect, if not by necessary connection, at least by custom and constant conjunction; that the sun will always rise tomorrow. Well, it doesn't and it won't, necessarily.

I was working from home at that time. I had built a new house near the old croft house and was living on my own. I had a long-haired cat called Sguab, a Gaelic word meaning 'sweep.' I have no idea how old Sguab was, as we got her when an old lady in Oban had passed away. I have to mention this cat as she is an important, even a vital, element in the story. The house was rather isolated. I had two neighbours, each of their houses about 150 metres away and I seldom had visitors.

Every day I would go to the village shop, a few miles away, for the daily newspaper. It was between 12 and 1pm and I was sitting in the living-room reading the paper and with the front door open. Suddenly I heard 3 or 4 distinct footsteps on the gravel outside. I immediately thought it was the lady next door. She would sometimes come with home baking, her way of thanking me for giving her a lift to Portree sometimes. I went to meet her at the front door but there was nobody there. I walked round the house to make sure. Nobody.

I went back to reading the paper. The incident disturbed me a little. I had read about auditory hallucinations and how they can be a symptom of mental disease. Was I going mad? I would have to wait and see, for that was the first time something like that had happened to me and if it was a symptom of such, it would surely occur more than once. So I assured myself. And yet I worried. Strangely enough, it was the cat who gave me the reassurance!

An hour or so later I was working at the computer in another room from which I could see Sguab sitting about 8 metres from me. She was facing the front door which was open and 4 metres distant. Suddenly, she went berserk. Her hair stood on end and she made the most awful noise I have ever heard from an animal. It was as if she was petrified. I ran and picked her up. The first thought that came to me was that it was a dog. I immediately looked outside. Nothing. I went round the house again to make sure there was nothing there. There wasn't anything to be seen.

I was baffled and rather frightened at what had happened. When you hear people talking of ghosts or read about them in books or see them in films, you think, O, yes, what a good story. But when it happens to yourself, to a sceptic, it is a different matter. This had the power to upset my world view. Things like that just shouldn't happen. The fact that Sguab had apparently seen something at least reassured me that, whatever it was, I was not the only one to have experienced it. Naturally, I linked the earlier footsteps I had heard with what the cat had apparently seen. This meant that what I had experienced was not subjective. Something had been at that door and the cat had experienced it. This assured me that the experience I had was most probably objective.

Some months after this incident, poor Sguab became ill with a virus and died. At the time I didn't connect her death with the 'ghost' incident. But some years later in Gairloch, when I was back teaching, I came across a story in a Gaelic course book on the subject of *manadh*. *Manadh* is a Gaelic word meaning a supernatural omen, apparition or warning. The story, as I recall it, was of a man who had been out at sea in a small boat and he had heard screaming as if someone was drowning. He took this to be a *manadh*. He took it so much to heart that he refused to go in a boat after that. Many years later it appears that he forgot his vow and on that very trip he was drowned.

When I read the story, I thought, could what happened that day in Staffin have been a kind of *manadh*? The incident might appear trivial in the grand scheme of things, but for a person of my disposition who was so sceptical and more disposed to believe in naturalism, it was a wake-up call. Synchronistic happenings, the intuitive appreciation of the miracle of things, the sense of the numinous, the sense of the whole-forming and self-organisation of matter from the galaxy to the cell – all these and now this were the beginnings of the proof I needed that naturalism is simply wrong.

Questions which I didn't ask at the time but which I ask myself now are: Was the Transcendent softening me for what was to come? Were all these years of seeking and questioning a prelude for what Transcendence in an amazing manner would reveal? '... our indiscretion sometimes serves us well, / When our brief plots do pall: and that should learn us / There's a divinity that shapes our ends, / Rough-hew them how we will ...' says Hamlet. And why indeed shouldn't Transcendence shape our ends? Although *we* (by the very nature of the case) cannot know what Transcendence is, except in as far as it reveals itself, why should not the ground of Being know and be able to affect what it has created?

If God indeed were to communicate with us at a personal level, how are we to recognize it as a message from him? Three things, first, we would have to believe there is a God in the first place in order for us to believe that it is he who is communicating with us. Second, we would have to be seekers after him and, third, the communication will likely be a surprise and completely confound our rationalism.

To my amazement, and I write as a former sceptic, I believe, looking over the course of my life, that God has communicated with me in ways that I couldn't have envisaged. Here I refer particularly to what happened in 2008–09 which I describe in Chapters 13 and 14. I realise this is a huge claim. Parts of the 'communication', of course, are things which are available to all open-minded people such as the latest discoveries of science, the sense of the numinous and so on. The other part is the personal part and I realize that I cannot prove that: it has to be taken on trust. The only other witness to what happened was my wife and it is to our story that I now return.

As Margaret mentioned, I finally split up with my girlfriend at the end of 2000. I was on my own and spent most of my time in Gairloch. Previously I would go back to Staffin at weekends. Now it was more convenient to stay on in Gairloch. I had not forgotten Margaret and, whatever prompted me to do so, I phoned her in May 2001. This was on a Friday evening. She said she had sent me a postcard that very day. Sure enough it arrived in the post next day. That was the first time we had communicated since the autumn of 2000. Another meaningful coincidence?

But let Margaret tell her side of the story.

• 8 •

St Kilda to Gairloch

My work as nurse in Benbecula and St Kilda continued as usual. But, strangely enough, so did the concern I had for Myles, although I felt it was easier to pray for him, as I now knew a little about his life and circumstances. I knew he wasn't a Christian. He had his own life to live and I had mine, although I would pray for him and I hoped in some way our meeting would have been of some help to him in his spiritual searching. As the months went by I didn't know whether I would ever see him again. The dream had troubled me for years and I felt, and even knew, that it was from God. I had to leave matters in his hands. If we met again it would be the Lord's doing.

Once again it was my turn to do my week's stint in St Kilda, a place where I felt the Lord to be very close to me. While I was there I felt something telling me that I should send Myles a postcard. At the same time I was reluctant to do so as he might take it the wrong way if I sent him a card. However, I knew that I had to be obedient to get relief from this concern once again, so I bought a postcard in the Scottish National Heritage shop and wrote on it ready for posting.

I left St Kilda and didn't post the card. But I couldn't sleep. For two nights, Wednesday and Thursday, I couldn't sleep, and I knew why. On Friday morning I posted the card. I was exhausted. Myles phoned me that night.

'I posted a card to you this morning,' I said.

'Did you?' He sounded surprised, probably as surprised as I was that he had phoned.

He invited me to join him in Gairloch for a function at a local hotel in aid of a local charity. I had an off-duty weekend and I accepted his invitation. I booked in at the hotel for a couple of nights. The evening function was very enjoyable. There was a buffet followed by a raffle and it gave me a chance to meet Myles's friends. On the Saturday afternoon I had visited him in the schoolhouse. We sat on the couch in the living room looking out the window at his dog, a springer spaniel, romping about in the garden while the cat was doing its best to avoid the dog.

We were all in a jovial mood. Myles started composing nonsense verses in Gaelic about a 'bodach' (an old man) and a 'cailleach' (an old woman) and various animals. Pure Edward Lear. The first verse went something like this: A bodach and a cailleach looking at a tree / and a kitten and a puppy beside them; / all they would now want would be the deil of a calf / and the house would be tapsalteerie. The verses went on about the antics of the animals and became more and more nonsensical. Good clean fun. However, the calf later played a part in the story as we shall see.

As I left Gairloch on the Monday, we kissed goodbye and I really didn't want that to happen. It made me wonder if it was the start of a relationship. By the time I had reached Lochcarron, about 50 miles from Gairloch, I needed a break and stopped for a coffee at a cafe and shop. As I was drinking my coffee I thought about the nonsense poem and especially the calf. I wondered whether they sold calf ornaments in the shop. It would be fun to get one as a memento of my visit to Gairloch and I also thought, probably foolishly, that it would the sign of the beginning of a relationship with Myles.

I had a look around the adjacent shop. Plenty other animal ornaments, but no calves. Disappointment. I asked the assistant and she went to the back store and returned with a red porcelain calf. I bought it and, to my surprise, I was quite thrilled. I carried on to Benbecula and later that evening telephoned Myles and told him of my experience.

Marriage

When Margaret phoned me on her return to Benbecula and mentioned the incident of the calf, I was rather amused. I cannot remember if I had told her about my study of Jung and synchronistic events at that stage or not. I might have done. What I found slightly amusing was that the idea of buying a calf had arisen from the nonsense verses I had composed extempore on Saturday. For me, the assistant finding a calf in the back store was not really a synchronistic event and for the simple reason that human will had entered into the equation. Margaret had decided to buy a calf and there happened to be a calf in the shop. So what? A synchronistic event for me had to be entirely spontaneous and unpredictable and outwith the control of the human will, like what had happened to me with the poem, 'Mending the Road.'

But Margaret had taken this for a sign and for the fun of it I decided to play along with the idea. 'Ok,' I said, 'if I see a red calf on or near the road when I'm going back to Staffin next weekend, I'll take that as a sign as well. I wasn't really treating the matter seriously; it was a bit of a joke. At the weekend as I travelled the 120 miles back to Staffin I kept my eyes open for red calves! I saw some in the distance, but none on or near the road. As I approached Staffin I had more or less given up the search. Less than a mile from home, as I went up the brae at Brogaig a car was stopped in front of me and I had to stop too. The cause of the stoppage was a number of red cattle, including 4 or 5 red calves, being guided across the road to another field. Needless to say, the joke was on me after all! Should I take this as a sign that a relationship should start? Who knows, but, whether justified or not, I did treat it as a case of meaningful coincidence.

From my point of view, that wouldn't have been a reason for starting a relationship. It would have been the least of reasons. On the other hand, Margaret's dream, and the effect the dream had on her, I was willing to take as a spiritual sign, for I could see that Margaret was a spiritual person. Imperfect, like myself and every other human being, but nevertheless a person who appeared to have a relationship with God. That impressed me. I could see that she had a completely different experience to me in religious matters. She didn't question things the way I did. One could say she was more normal!

After leaving home and in her twenties and thirties she ignored God and couldn't make sense of religion. And then she went through some hard times in her life and had a conversion experience. She didn't have the intellectual struggles that I had, always questioning, questioning, questioning. She had no interest in philosophy or science as they relate to religious questions; nor indeed did she have an interest in contemporary poetry. Before she met me, if someone had asked what she thought of modern Gaelic poetry, she would have replied, 'A load of rubbish.'

That didn't faze me in the least. I was after all familiar with *The Varieties of Religious Experience* by William James and with *Mysticism: The Nature and Development of Spiritual Consciousness* by Evelyn Underhill. To meet a person who had had genuine personal experiences as described in these two books was for me of profound significance. That such a person should have had a mysterious and powerful dream about me was for me a humbling experience. Though I could see that we had very different personalities and didn't share the same understanding of religion, I was still drawn to her and even felt that she had been sent into my life by the Transcendent, for whatever reason. The fact that she had a strong, simple faith in God in contrast to my Herculean struggles with doubt made her even more attractive.

We started going together and I visited her in Benbecula. We were engaged at Christmas of that year and married in April 2002.

'Are you doing the right thing?'

Before we married (Margaret recalls), one thing which I did learn about Myles was that he was a fairly well-known Gaelic poet. I wasn't a reader of poetry, so had no idea what he had written. The local minister, however, did know because he had studied Myles's poetry for Higher Gaelic. Naturally he wasn't impressed with what Myles believed, as that came through in the poetry. When he heard that we were getting married he visited twice and asked me to consider carefully the step I was taking and was I quite sure I was doing the right thing. He was, of course, doing this with the best of intentions for he knew that I was a professing Christian and he thought I wouldn't be very happy married to a poet who was an unbeliever.

I prayed that I was doing the right thing. As our relationship developed, the worry I had felt left me and the tears stopped. Then eventually there came my last trip to St Kilda and once again the earnest prayer. One evening as I was lying on my bed just talking to God about it all, he gave me a vision of Myles lying on a couch and with that the words, 'His needs are greater than yours.' That was definite proof for me that I was doing the right thing and that God was going before me.

• 9 •

Intuition and the greater self

Jung's four functional types

The poet's way, and, indeed, most people's way of coming to the 'truth' about life and 'reality' is to be naturally soaked in that truth and life, very often without thinking about it.

Jung usefully talks of 'four functional types' when it comes to the way people orientate themselves to experience. The four functions are sensation, feeling, thinking and intuition. Some people think and analyse life a lot. Others get by more on feeling, that is, they make value judgements, for example, whether things are good or bad, agreeable or disagreeable. Sensation is to do with perceiving what your sense organs are telling you. Intuition is having a 'hunch' about something. Sensation and intuition Jung describes as irrational functions and he goes on to say: 'Intuition is more like a sense-perception, which is also an irrational event in so far as it depends essentially upon objective stimuli, which owe their existence to physical and not mental causes.'[1]

Both feeling and thinking, on the other hand, he categorizes as rational, that is, ordering functions of the mind. In addition, he makes clear, '... that these four criteria of types of human behaviour are just four viewpoints among many others, like will power, temperament, imagination, memory, and so on.'[2]

I find Jung's four criteria useful when thinking on how we acquire knowledge. For some people thinking is important, often at the expense of other means of experiencing. For others, intuition is more important. They weigh up a situation intuitively and act accordingly. Such people are acutely aware of people's body language and facial expressions.

It is sometimes said that the poet is the same as anyone else, only more sensitive. I think this makes sense. Ideally, the poet will be fine-tuned

53

in all four criteria, that is, acutely aware of the world of the senses, the world of feeling or value judgements, the world of the intellect and of his intuitions. It seems to me now, and maybe I was not always aware enough of it, that science and reason excluded a whole swathe of what is most valuable in human experience, and has nothing important to say about the most important things in life. John C. Lennox, who is himself a scientist, thinks 'the claim' (by people like Richard Dawkins) 'that only science can deliver truth' to be completely mistaken. If it were so it would mean the abandonment of much of what is studied in universities including 'philosophy, literature and art and music.' Science cannot prove whether a poem or a painting is good or bad. It cannot tell 'whether a painting is a masterpiece or a confused smudge of colours ... by making a chemical analysis of the paint on the canvas.'[3] The same is true of morality.

Science has nothing to say about those things which make us most human: the appreciation of sensory qualities such as colour tones and sound tones; the awareness of beauty; the awareness of the intrinsic values of things and, perhaps most of all, the ability to appreciate the wholeness of a scene, a painting, a poem or piece of music.

This feeling for wholeness and the conviction that there is a natural whole-forming foundation to art, to life and to the very structure of the universe is of vital significance to anyone who seeks to find meaning in life.

The poet senses this wholeness by using all faculties possible, including imagination. Intuition and feeling might give a hint. Imagination – not in the sense of fancy but a much more basic faculty of the mind – enables the thousand suggestions of intuition and feeling to be drawn together. The life of the seeking poet is a journey and indeed may go from a life dominated by sensation to a life where another function might dominate. A poem I wrote in the late 1990s was influenced by Jung's four categories and illustrates the different stages a person might be at. The following is a translation:

The five Natures

I'm the flesh, stroked by desire, / a wanton kite, up and down in the storm; / I can't escape the devil's low grasp.

I'm the rational, who has to be decent; / the world requires we don't yield to the beast; / keep to the rule and you'll have happiness and wealth.

I'm the moral, duty is written on my heart; / desire is subjugated, I detest lust and discord; / keeping the rules saves our lives from the mob.

I'm intuition's progeny, governed by depth, / sons and daughters of God, of best conduct; / we must be obedient, loving and honouring each other.

I'm the mystic, who has met the Being behind self; / awe and dread are in my face; / I've seen and felt the wholeness of the stars.[4]

This poem was suggested by Jung's four types of human behaviour, but it also rang true for my own experience and I believe it might ring true for the experience of others. When I was young and a believer in naturalism, the sensual and rational modes dominated my life. Of course, no-one, or comparatively few, will be at the mercy of one mode of being and most people will, for example, have moral constraints and a feeling for what is right and wrong. But many people will be dominated by one or two ways of being and many people will not progress beyond the first two ways. Although the poem does suggest that there can be a movement and a maturing in the psyche as one ages, what Jung terms 'individuation.'

The fifth and mystical stage is linked to the vision given by the Dutch philosopher, Herman Dooyeweerd (1894–1977) of a cosmic unity given to us all potentially in and through our experience and mediated through intuition and what he calls the 'supratemporal heart.' Dooyeweerd has been called 'the most original philosopher Holland has ever produced, even Spinoza not excepted.'[5] (He himself, however, stressed the continuity of his work with mainstream western philosophy and that he was examining the roots and development of western philosophy.) His major works have been translated into English, for example, the four-volume *A New Critique of Theoretical Thought* in 1953. For him, what the Bible calls the 'heart' is what potentially links us to the eternal and to transcendent.

Jung's greater self

There is according to Jung a centre in each person which he calls the Self and, if allowed to, this 'organising centre' will through dreams encourage the maturation of the individual through the stages of life. M.-L. Von Franz gives a fascinating account of the role played by what they called *Mista'peo* or 'Great Man' in the life of the Naskapi tribe of the Labrador peninsula. In Jung's day they are described as 'hunters who live in isolated family groups.' The 'Great Man' revealed himself to the Naskapi through dreams. Those who paid close attention to their dreams could 'enter into a deeper connection with the Great Man.' The individual had a duty to follow what he was told in his dreams and transmute them into art. The dreams enable the Naskapi to find their 'way in life' both spiritually and practically, with the weather, for example, and in their hunting.[5]

Von Franz goes on to explain that this Self of the dreams is different from the conscious self and helps the individual to extend and mature the personality. It first appears as 'an inborn possibility' and may develop ever so slightly or more completely. Its development will depend on the willingness of 'the ego to listen to the messages of the Self.'[6]

A number of important points arise from Jung's analysis of the life of the psyche from the Naskapi example. It shows what is potentially the most profound case of whole-forming in the whole of creation, the journey of the soul or the inner self in the process of individuation or maturing. Just as the body realises its potential for growth and development from childhood to maturity and then the decline into old age, so the inner life of the soul can develop and mature, if allowed and prompted to do so. Just as the body needs nourishment in order to grow, so the soul needs its own nourishment.

Was this not what Jesus meant when he said, 'What good will it be for a man if he gains the whole world, yet forfeits his soul? Or what can a man give in exchange for his soul?'[7] Or as it says in the gospel of John, 'The true light that gives light to every man was coming into the world.'[8] The true light, the Logos, is in all but we have to notice that it's there and act on it if we are to mature as souls. This same truth is even more clearly spelled out in the parable of the sower who went out to sow seed. Some fell by the path and the birds ate it up, some fell among rocks and although it sprang up quickly the sun soon withered it, other seed fell among thorns which choked the plants, while, finally, seeds fell on good soil and produced a crop – a hundred, sixty or thirty times what was sown. Of course the Master himself is the grain and the light and the seed, the universal Logos, the eternal possibility of growth and wholeness, or what Dooyeweerd calls 'the new root.'

To go back to the poem I quoted earlier, 'The Five Types', the five verses mark out possible stages a soul can be at. The first one is of the earth, earthly and the person who is at this stage is lost in the world of desire and probably engrossed with the world of the material. The second-stage person, the rational, has taken stock and from a point of view which might be of self-interest, realises society requires that desires be subjugated to social rules. This is an improvement on the potential licentiousness of the first stage.

The third-stage person realises that morality is not merely social rules and enlightened self-interest but is something more profound. He or she might even realise that duty comes from moral laws written into the fabric of the universe or given in a rule book, whether the Bible or Koran or some other holy book, issuing from a lawgiver. In such a person there is strong feeling for what is morally right.

At the fourth stage there is the dawning of a sense of awe, the realisation that virtue is its own reward. That agape love – that is, Christian love – is more important even than duty. Indeed, that to love in this way *is* our duty. That it is important to love and respect other human beings individually and as members of the human family, because in some meaningful way they are made in the image of the creator.

The fourth stage of the soul's journey merges into the fifth stage which is a uniting of all that has been learnt from the four previous stages. All the insights gained from the senses and from intellectual exploration, from multitudinous intuitions and feeling judgements; from experiences with other people and places, from wide-ranging and deep reflection; particularly from a feeling for the wholeness and unity of all things. All these come together in the consciousness to create in the person a feeling of tremendous awe in the face of the primal reality. The whole of nature and reality are impregnated with a feeling of the numinous, which I discuss in the next chapter.

To my mind Dooyeweerd's idea of the 'supratemporal heart', Jung's idea of the 'greater self' and Rudolph Otto's idea of the numinous are closely linked. They all relate to a transcendent reality.

• 10 •

Rudolph Otto and the numinous

The 'numinous' is an adjective coined by Rudolph Otto in the book
Das Heilige, published in English as *The Idea of the Holy,* from the
Latin 'numen' meaning 'the divine will; the might of a deity, majesty,
divinity.' Otto needed a word to convey the powerful, irrational feeling
felt by some people in the face of the inexplicable and the supernatural.
God is described by the churches in rational terms using concepts such
as 'Spirit, Reason, Purpose, Good Will, Supreme Power, Unity, Selfhood.'
But Otto thinks it is 'seriously misleading' to think of God *only* in this
way. There is another side to Deity which 'require(s) comprehension of
a quite different kind' and 'completely eludes apprehension in terms
of concepts.' It is linked to the feeling of the 'holy' and gives rise to a
'numinous state of mind' which is 'perfectly *sui generis* and irreducible
to any other.' Further, this state of mind 'cannot, strictly speaking, be
taught, it can only be evoked, awakened in the mind ...'[1] Furthermore,
the numinous is felt as a presence and is felt as objective and outside
the self.

In an effort to describe what is, in effect, a special feeling, Otto uses
certain terms such as 'creature-feeling', *mysterium tremendum* and
fascinans. Creature-feeling is 'the note of self-abasement into nothingness
before an overpowering, absolute might of some kind' as when Abraham
pleads with God for the men of Sodom and says, 'Behold now, I have
taken upon me to speak into the Lord, which am but dust and ashes.'[2]
Words Otto uses to speak of the *tremendum* are 'peculiar dread', 'a terror
fraught with inward shuddering', 'awe', 'dread', 'uncanny', 'eerie', 'weird',
'the Wrath of Yahweh', 'absolute inapproachability', 'majesty.' All these
terms of course are analogies used to try and describe Something which
is wholly other and in the end indescribable.

The mysterium is 'wholly other', 'mystery', 'stupor' which 'signifies blank wonder, and astonishment that strikes us dumb, amazement absolute':

> The truly 'mysterious' object is beyond our apprehension and comprehension, not only because our knowledge has certain irremovable limits, but because in it we come upon something inherently 'wholly other', whose kind and character are incommensurable with our own, and before which we therefore recoil in a wonder that strikes us chill and dumb.[3]

How different is this approach to that of scientists who advocate naturalism, for example, Professor of Ecology and Evolution Massimo Pigiucci who is reported as saying: 'The basic assumption of science is that the world can be explained entirely in physical terms, without recourse to godlike entities.'[4]

Interestingly, Otto identifies the awareness of the divine with Mysticism and he says:

> We come upon the ideas, first, of the annihilation of self, and then, as its complement, of the transcendent as the sole and entire reality. These are the characteristic notes of Mysticism in all its forms, however otherwise various in content. For one of the chiefest and most general features of Mysticism is just this self-depreciation (so plainly parallel in the case of Abraham), the estimation of the self, of the personal 'I', as something not perfectly or essentially real, or even as a mere nullity ... And on the other hand Mysticism leads to a valuation of the transcendent object of its reference as that which through plenitude of being stands supreme and absolute, so that the finite self contrasted with it becomes conscious even in its nullity that 'I am nought, Thou art all.'[5]

And he makes an interesting comparison with Buddhism when he says 'the 'void' of the eastern, like the 'nothing' of the western mystic is a numinous ideogram of the 'wholly other.'

I have described Otto's categories at some length because they appear to link with what was happening to me in the 1990s in the years leading up to meeting and marrying Margaret. I was becoming more and more aware of a divine unity behind appearances. I had a sense of awe and at the same time a sense self-deprecation. In my 1994 poetry collection *A' Gabhail Ris* (Accepting) there is a poem, of which this is a translation:

Song

I saw the sun rising / like an innocent globe in the sky ...

Chorus: and I was seized with dread/awe.

I saw the little birds / with their skilful responses ...

I saw how you loved me / although I didn't always understand it ...

I saw the adults / how they killed their own kind ...

I saw I could never fathom it / although I lived to be a hundred ...

I saw the imposing stability / in the atoms of the waves ...

I saw that in the dark brine / there is no feeling for the drowned ...

I saw the incredible speed / of light travelling through space ...

I saw the distress / suffered unexpectedly ...

I saw you, world of graces / turning like a jewel in space ...

I remembered what Scripture said, / the fear of God, the beginning of wisdom ...[6]

This fear, this *tremendum*, which Otto so graphically suggests and for which the word 'fear' in its anthropological sense is only a pale and insufficient comparison, was beginning to grip my soul. It is more than mere fear. It is a stupor, an amazement at how anything at all should be; a bowing down before the miracle, the terror, the necessity, the contingency of creation; an instinctive belief, a crying out, that this just couldn't happen on its own, that it needs a creator – a Mind which has given it its intelligibility, not the human mind which is a temporal phenomenon, but a divine, eternal mind.

Creature-consciousness

Part of Otto's mysterium-tremendum, is the contrast of the Creator with the creature. He calls this 'creature-consciousness' or 'creature-feeling.' It cannot be explained conceptually, but has to be felt. All it can express

> ... is the note of self-abasement into nothingness before an overpowering, absolute might of some kind; whereas everything turns on the **character** of this overpowering might, a character which cannot be expressed verbally, and can only be suggested indirectly through the tone and content of a man's feeling-response to it. And this response must be directly experienced in oneself to be understood.[7] (author's emphasis)

According to Otto, this is not merely a feeling of 'self-depreciation' or even of *self*-consciousness. As if one was conceiving or valuing oneself as being nothing, using concepts, in relation to a greater power. Rather, this feeling is related to 'an object outside the self' and is directly related to the spontaneously felt power which he calls the numinous. 'The numinous', he says, 'is thus felt as objective and outside the self.' The 'numen' is experienced as being present.

Without contesting Otto's argument in any way for a directly felt numinous presence, there are other considerations which may complement his insight. The awareness of a Creator is brought home at the beginning of the 21st century by the discoveries of science in the last hundred years. I am thinking of discoveries, already mentioned, in the fields of cosmology and microbiology. The vastness and fine-tuning in the starry cosmos and the incredible intricacies of cell biology. There is also the inexorable uni-directionality of time's arrow. The movement of the stars and galaxies are all part of this universal movement. And, closer to home, the movement of every living thing is a steady progress to disintegration and death. This realisation of the link human life and death have with the inevitable movement of the cosmos is a sobering thought.

This indescribable vastness of space-time and the absolute vulnerability and puny insignificance of the human makes us gasp. As the psalmist says in the eighth psalm when he considered the starry heavens, 'What is man that thou art mindful of him?' How much more can we say this in the

21st century? It is not only the vastness of space-time which amazes us but the deep mystery of it. What is there at the edge of space? If we could travel at the speed of light until we came to its edge, what would we find? No doubt science has some explanation, for example, that, if we carried on forever, we would come back to where we started from, for they tell us that space is curved.

But no, that's not what I meant. What I meant was that as a person living in three-dimensional space and using my 'normal' imagination, I cannot conceive what there is 'outside' the space I inhabit. There is something strange and completely mysterious about it. Outside space is outwith my imagination! What this 'outside' is which human imagination is not fitted to fathom, we can have no idea. But there are hints, as we have seen, that three-dimensional space is only part of the story, that there is a reality which transcends us and our time-space habitat.

All these thoughts and feelings combined in me, with Otto's sense of the numinous, to produce a feeling-complex difficult to describe. Some of these feelings come through in a poem I wrote around the time Margaret and I met for the second time. Here is a translation:

The Worm

1. A worm / in the soil of the world, / I sometimes, I think, feel a warmth / as if a hand were stroking me. / Sometimes above me / I feel footsteps / without pause, / ceaseless, / but one day / as if something disturbed the soil / I was thrown upwards / and an unknown glow burnt my back.

I wish I was / back in the soil / feeling the gentle finger / agitating me / stroking me / with the knowledge of the distant light, high above me.

2. Even the worm / can feel the weight of the god.

Even the worm / can recognise the heat of the sun.[8]

Like all religious language, this is analogous. The worm is the lowest form of life; the sun is an analogy for the Source of all life. I remember feeling at the time the tremendous gift, that is, life, that I had been given.

Supposing I was utterly mortal and that there was no afterlife, yet I should be supremely thankful that the Lord of life should have revealed the miracle of his creation to me, even if only for a fleeting moment. I felt the gulf, the utter gulf, and at the same time the sheer ecstasy. The ecstasy of being alive in the presence of his creation.

Another poem on the same theme attempts to capture my utter amazement that a person as sinful and as unworthy as I was should be having the experiences that I was having. The stone is an analogy for the hardness and scepticism of my heart:

The Breaking of the Stone

You built a dwelling, glory, / in my heart, / although unaware you were building it. / O invisible marvel of the spirit! / In the midst of the mire and the mud / your hands / most white / were preparing the site / something inexplicable / inscrutable / unbelievable.

Ah! The stone is still there / keeping you out, / a great brute of a stone where a path should be.

Break it, glory / although painful, break it / in smithereens / until there is a smooth path, at last, / for your foot / and I will hear the sound of your feet on the gravel

and with awe and dread / I'll wait your glorious arrival.

And the once empty house / will be full of amazing furniture, / full, full, full, / and it will be nothing.[9]

The poem describes in a small way the awareness of the glory of a transcendent God; it is a feeling of the heart. Yet, at the same time, there was the 'great brute of stone' keeping me from fully accepting the true reality of God in my life. The stone represents doubt. I was still under the influence of naturalism and deeply aware of the juggernaut of the one-way arrow of time. Reason told me that when life ended and the body went into the grave, that that was that. *Finis*. End of story.

It would take even more than I had experienced up until then to finally convince me that naturalism was wrong and that what appeared self-evident was not so self-evident after all. It had been a long journey – this search for the truth about life which had started in my teens. It appeared that 'The Hound of Heaven' was following me and, despite all my betrayals, would not let me go. The first verse of Francis Thompson's poem spoke and still speaks loudly to me:

> *I fled Him, down the nights and down the days; / I fled Him, down the arches of the years; / I fled Him, down the labyrinthine ways / Of my own mind; and in the midst of tears / I hid from Him, and under running laughter. / Up vistaed hopes I sped; / And shot, precipitated, / Adown Titanic glooms of chasmed fears, / From those strong Feet that followed, followed after. / But with unhurrying chase, / And unperturbéd pace, / Deliberate speed, majestic instancy, / They beat – and a Voice beat / More instant than the Feet – / 'All things betray thee, who betrayest Me.'*[10]

The fact that I had betrayed him, but that yet he was still following me would become ever clearer.

• 11 •

Nature as miracle

Poetic and scientific truth

Before Margaret phoned me out of the blue to Staffin, I had been staying there a number of years, first of all working on writing projects, mainly teaching materials for Gaelic learners. And then in 1996 I went back to High School teaching and ended up in Gairloch, Wester Ross. Often I would drive the two and a half hours home to Staffin for the weekend. The schoolhouse where I stayed in Gairloch was beside the school and it was a relief to get away from the precincts for a couple of days.

In these days, in the early and mid nineties I continued to write poetry. Poetry for me has always been an expression of life. It has to have integrity and it has to have vision. As I have tried to show, the poet is like a sponge soaking in all kinds of influences and ideas and distilling these million promptings to create his own truth. There is a kind of sixth sense at work: a hint given by the senses will change everything. A drop of a different colour will change the colour of the whole liquid. The poet must take things as they are, however uncomfortable.

The scientist works in a similar way, in working from hypothesis to theory, weighing and measuring experience and throwing out the theory if the evidence doesn't fit. But, of course, there is a vital difference, for the scientist accepts only certain types of evidence, that which in an experiment can be weighed and measured and which, vitally, can be repeated. On the other hand, not all science is like that, cosmology for instance. The cosmologist cannot create the conditions of the original creation event in the laboratory, but he does study the evidence. He uses another method which, according to John C. Lennox, 'is an essential part of the methodology of science', namely, 'the method of inference' to work out what the best explanation is for what is presented to the senses. Thus applying the inferential method to events which happen only once, it is still possible to ask what the best explanation for these events is. The logic of it is: 'If A, then B is likely.'[1]

This sounds suspiciously like the method of the artist or poet, but in his case the sifting of the evidence is more comprehensive. It is sifted through the web of his life and consciousness and the conclusion is arrived at by a process of osmosis. The 'truth' of the true poem is this sort of truth, a truth obtained by a process of refinement, a truer truth than science because it doesn't ignore the large swathes of experience which happen only once. It doesn't ignore the vital personal element, including purposive activity. The poet, or at least the kind of poet I am thinking of, will not discard any evidence. For that which happened only once, has nevertheless happened.

For me the creation of art is potentially a link with the transcendent and therefore a kind of miracle.

The hidden Christ

The subjects I taught in Gairloch High School were Gaelic and Religious Education. The RE course was eclectic and encouraged pupils to explore six major world religions – Christianity, Buddhism, Islam, Hinduism, Sikhism and Judaism. The emphasis was on exploring the world faiths for themselves and then letting pupils make up their own minds what they believed. Certainly, my view at the time was that all faiths have valuable insights into the human condition, and that is still my view. The objection I had to the doctrine of Election when I was a youngster was that it seemed to condemn most of the human race to hell. I prefer to believe in a loving God who judges the heart, something other human beings are incapable of, simply because they are not privy to other people's innermost thoughts and feelings. Only an omniscient transcendent being could have such knowledge.

The New Testament certainly seems to point to a single way to salvation, for example, where Jesus says, 'I am the way, the truth and the life'[2] or 'Therefore Jesus said again, "I tell you the truth, I am the gate for the sheep. All whoever came before me were thieves and robbers, but the sheep did not listen to them. I am the gate; whoever enters through me will be saved."'[3] This implies that Jesus is the one way to God. And if so, the question arises what happened to the millions of people who never heard the Gospel or the people who belong to other religions?

It appears to me that the Apostle Paul gives the answer. First, he asserts that for people anywhere it is self-evident from nature that there is a God: 'For since the creation of the world God's invisible qualities – his eternal power and divine nature – have been clearly seen, being understood from what has been made, so that men are without excuse.'[4] Furthermore, the Jews were given the law to live by but the non-Jews 'are a law for themselves, even though they do not have the law, since they show that the requirements of the law are written on their hearts, their consciences also bearing witness, and their thoughts now accusing, now even defending them.'[5] Later he says, 'What shall we say? That the Gentiles, who did not pursue righteousness, have obtained it, a righteousness that is by faith ...'[6]

In other words, there is what I like to call the hidden Christ. It is part of being human to have the possibility of knowing good from evil and in the end the human being is judged by his own conscience and in the end by the Logos, the Christ who was with God in the creation of the universe. As it is famously put in John's gospel:

> In the beginning was the Word, and the word was with God, and the Word was God. He was with God in the beginning. Through him all things were made; without him nothing was made that has been made. In him was life, and that life was the light of men. That light shines in the darkness, but the darkness has not understood it.[7]

In other words, the Logos, the Son of God, made the world and is in every human heart, although all people might not recognise the Logos within. This answers the question regarding other peoples and religions that I had as a child. God knows his own, whatever tribe or religion they belong to. That also is part of the miracle of creation.

Miracles and the supernatural

When I was in Gairloch, I still wasn't at the stage where I could completely accept the Christian message. By that I mean to accept the resurrection of Jesus as a fact. For it seems to me that the resurrection is a central part of the Christian message. As the great apostle to the gentiles said, writing to the Corinthians: 'And if Christ has not been raised, our preaching is useless and so is your faith.'[8] At that stage of my life I was not willing to accept the reality of anything supernatural or miraculous because I was still strongly influenced by a naturalistic world view. I reasoned to myself, When you're dead, you're dead. The body rots and decays and mental life is tied to the body. In what conceivable way could the human personality survive the dissolution of the body?

It would be years before I would become convinced that there is in fact life after death. What precise form that life takes I have no idea. But I am quite certain that there is some form of afterlife and the belief in an afterlife is strongly linked to the belief in a creator God. You cannot have one without the other. As I said at the start, this book is really the story of how I became convinced that there is a transcendent reality that we call God and the different elements that led to this change of view.

As far as the interpretation of reality in terms of natural / supernatural is concerned, the resurrection, in fact, is the great arbiter. It is a lightning strike, splitting off the believer in supernatural explanations from the believer in naturalistic explanations. For the heirs of David Hume and the enlightenment, the resurrection is unbelievable. It is a miracle, and miracles just don't happen. Hugh Montefiore is a Jew who converted to Christianity, and who was a New Testament scholar in the University of Cambridge and Bishop of Birmingham from 1978 to 1987. He considers how some people reject all miracles and takes Hume as an example.

For Hume the so-called laws of nature were 'only universally observed uniformities.' A miracle would mean a breach of these uniformities and they would not then be universal. There would need to be greater evidence for a breach of these uniformities than there is for uniformity. Hume did not think such evidence had ever been produced. Therefore, miracles do not happen, 'although the possibility of their occurrence is not entirely ruled out.'[9]

Hume, it has to be said, was writing in the 18th century and much has been discovered since then which casts doubt on the usefulness of what he has to say, particularly when it comes to the supernatural and miracles. He was an empiricist and one wonders what he would have made of recent discoveries in cosmology, quantum mechanics, biochemistry, near death experiences and so on. Discoveries which cast serious doubt on a naturalistic explanation of the universe.

Montefiore doesn't rule miracles out. How could he when it is clear that he believes in God and with God anything is possible? But it is clear that he is unhappy with miracles. When he was a lecturer, he 'tended to vacillate' and he thought miracles stories were 'legends, symbolic expressions of the spiritual ministry of Jesus or myths and stories that came into existence after his death.'[10] Later he changed his mind and came to believe that many of the miracles could be interpreted as 'paranormal' phenomena.

The resurrection appearances of Jesus he attributes to what he calls 'veridical hallucinations' which were 'truthful representations of his (that is, Jesus') spiritual presence in a visual form. They were veridical because the risen Christ really was spiritually present. The images formed were not internally generated, as in other kinds of hallucination, but were transferred to the brain by a form of telepathy.'[11]

Later he admits that such hallucinations 'only give us some kind of analogy of what happened in the case of Jesus' resurrection appearances.' And his book concludes with this rather ambiguous paragraph:

> Having concluded that the disciples did indeed see the risen Jesus, we are forced back on the question asked throughout this book: was this a purely supernatural event or did it make use of the paranormal phenomenon of veridical hallucination? It is noteworthy that there is **no mention of the supernatural in the Gospel accounts of the resurrection stories**, and a paranormal explanation is consistent with a critical examination of their contents.[12] (my highlighting)

No mention of the supernatural? Surely this begs the question? What could be more supernatural than someone coming back from the dead? And even by Montefiore's own definition of what the resurrection consisted of, namely, Jesus coming back to his disciples as a 'veridical hallucination', is that not a most significant supernatural event? Is it not just playing with words to call it 'paranormal'? And when does an event pass over from being a paranormal event to being a supernatural one?

A well-respected contemporary scholar in resurrection studies, Professor Gary R. Habermas of Liberty University, has no doubt that the resurrection of Jesus actually took place. In many scholarly studies he exposes the weaknesses of naturalistic explanations, and believes that alternative naturalistic theories fail to account for the historical facts. These evidences and a 'minimum facts' argument based on data agreed on by 'virtually all scholars' show 'conclusively' that the claims of the earliest eyewitnesses were as they claimed. 'Jesus was literally raised from the dead and appeared physically to a number of his followers, both individually and in groups.'[13]

In other words, God intervened in human history in what was a spectacular supernatural event. It has divided opinion ever since, even among theologians. Some like R. Bultmann, W. Marxsen and H. Koester, according to Habermas,[14] are shy of thinking of the resurrection in supernatural terms. Others, like Barth, think it should be accepted by faith because it cannot be verified historically. At the other end of the spectrum are theologians, mostly evangelicals, who believe in a corporeal resurrection and who represent the 'traditional, orthodox view.'

Personally, I think the scientific discoveries of the 20th and 21st centuries make it easier to believe in a supernatural event such as the resurrection. These discoveries, I feel, point to a supernatural source and disclose the universe to be pure miracle. Later in this book I will be looking at some of these discoveries in more detail, but first I would like to look at what is meant by 'miracle' and 'supernatural.'

My dictionary defines a miracle as 'an event contrary to the laws of nature and attributed to a supernatural cause.' While 'supernatural' is defined as 'of or relating to things that cannot be explained according to natural laws; of or caused as if by a god; miraculous; of or involving occult beings.'[15] There is an obvious overlap between the two terms, but a 'miracle' as defined here would obviously include such events as a spontaneous healing from an incurable disease or an object appearing in front of one out of thin air. It is something that happens outside of normal cause and effect. So miraculous events are by definition 'supernatural' in the sense that they cannot be explained by natural causes

'Supernatural' events such as poltergeist activity, ghostly visitations and so on cannot be explained either by natural causes. But the term 'natural causes' requires explanation. Usually by natural causes we mean causes that can be investigated by science and scientific methods. But there could be, and I for one believe there is, a realm beyond 'natural' causation with its own causality but which is not susceptible to scientific exploration. For me supernatural events are events that do occur but which cannot be verified scientifically, that is by repeated experiments, and for the very good reason that they only happen spontaneously and usually only once. The same goes for miracles.

One reason why I believe in the supernatural and even in the miraculous is that such events happened in my own life, events which I would describe as supernatural. I will recount some of these in this book. That such happened to me – and to Margaret – is one of the reasons why I have been forced to revise my world view.

'Miracle' in the sense of 'wonderful, amazing'

There is also another meaning of the word miraculous which is well worth considering, the meaning of 'wonderful, amazing, and marvellous.' An actual one-off miracle can inspire wonder and awe, but I really believe that the world in itself is a miracle, in both senses of the word, in fact the greatest miracle of all. I feel ashamed that it has taken me so long to appreciate the miracle which is the world. A miracle is something that cannot happen by itself. We attribute a miracle to a higher intelligence or cause. Of course, I often had a sense of wonder about the world, but for a long time I didn't fully realise just how wonderful it is. Part of this wonder is realising, finally and utterly, that this world requires an intelligence beyond our imagining for it to exist at all.

It always comes back to the question, 'Why is there something rather than nothing?' If there was but a drop of water in existence, it would still require an explanation. Where did it come from? Did it just come from nothing? How much more so does a universe of such amazing intricacy, and which has produced creatures that can think about it, demand an explanation. Some people might go through life without thinking and being amazed at the stupendous mystery of the existence of things. But the more science has discovered the more the mystery has deepened. The more amazed we become.

No-one better captures, describes and analyses this sense of wonder than Roy Abraham Varghese in his book *The Wonder of the World*, subtitled 'A Journey from Modern Science to the Mind of God.' Miracles, he says, 'are spoken of as exceptions to the laws of nature, but it seems obvious that the laws of nature themselves constitute the greatest miracles of all.'[16] Varghese has an insightful and informed grasp of what is involved. That there should be laws of nature at all is essential for the world to be intelligible to mind. Why are there laws in the first place and where did they come from? He considers the existence of these laws as 'the single greatest mystery uncovered by science.' Scientists such as Newton, Einstein and Hawking when considering such laws are led to the 'inescapable conclusion' that the laws of nature proceed from 'an infinite Intelligence, the Mind of God.'[17]

Einstein, for example, was of the opinion that anyone who looked deeply and seriously at the scientific evidence will be convinced 'that the laws of nature manifest the existence of a spirit vastly superior to that of human persons.'[18]

It is obvious to Varghese that supernaturalism in the form of theism beats any form of naturalism hands down. One of the most telling arguments he makes for a supreme intelligence is the extraordinary information systems that are part and parcel of biological systems. For instance, every cell of a human body contains 10^{12} bits of information, and each one of these cells has the information coded within it that makes it capable of duplicating the complete organism. How can such detailed information arise from unconscious matter by necessity and chance?

Faced with virtually thousands of special conditions needed in order for life to appear in the first place and the apparently spontaneous arrival of intricate information necessary for biological organisms, little wonder that many great scientific minds, indeed some of the greatest, are ready to admit that an intelligent Mind is a necessary precondition for the appearance of life. In 1992 Varghese co-edited a book with Henry Margenau in which leading scientists, including twenty Nobel Prize winners, were asked six questions including, What are your thoughts on the concept of God and on the existence of God?

While not claiming 'to being a statistically significant survey of the religious beliefs of modern scientists', nevertheless, some of the answers, coming as they do from some of the world's leading 20th century scientists, are intriguing. Here is a sample: 'How can I exist without a creator? I am not aware of any compelling answer ever given.'[19] (Professor Ulrich J. Becker) 'Appeal to God may be needed to answer the 'origin' question: Why should a quantum universe evolving towards a semi classical limit be consistent?'[20] (Professor Geoffrey F. Chew) 'I believe there is a God and that God brings structure to the universe on all levels from elementary particles to living beings to superclusters of galaxies.'[21] (Professor John Erik Fornaess) 'To me personally nothing is more evident, more certain, than the existence or reality of God.'[22] (Professor Wolfgang Smith)

Varghese's book, *The Wonder of the World*, intriguingly, may have played a part in the conversion to deism of one of Britain's best known atheists and an authority on Hume, the late Antony Flew. Flew, to the chagrin of the 'new atheists' such as Richard Dawkins and Daniel Dennett, described how he has changed his mind on the question of God's existence in the book *There is a God*. In an appendix he says that Varghese's book will need to be taken into account in any future discussion of God and philosophy. It 'provides an extremely extensive argument (sic) of the inductive argument from the order of nature.' Whether Varghese's book played a key role or not in Flew's change of mind, it is clear that new discoveries in science certainly did. A philosophical question that requires an answer is how 'a universe of mindless matter' could produce 'beings with intrinsic ends, self-replication capabilities, and 'coded chemistry'?[23]

At the beginning of the 21st century are we seeing what could be described as the New Enlightenment, side by side with the so-called 'new atheism.' Hume, as a philosopher, was at the centre of the first enlightenment. Is it possible that new insights being gained almost daily in cosmology, physics and biology are forcing philosophers and scientists to consider the inadequacy of naturalism as a philosophy? Many people, including leading thinkers, are asking whether the facts demand a supernatural explanation.

Life in Gairloch and my understanding of the Fall

Two views of sin

We lived in Gairloch for the first two years of our marriage. Margaret worked in an old folk's home and I worked in the local school. I had been going to church before we married and it appeared to me that there was a lot of emphasis on sin. Usually, I would count the number of times that the word 'sin' came up in the sermon. I still hadn't come to understand what sin was in its full significance, and the reason I didn't understand it was that I still thought of it in naturalistic terms. To really understand sin, one has to truly believe in God – in a God of absolute perfection and holiness. A God who can be in relational terms with humanity and with individual human beings.

I was still using my reason to understand sin and saw it in human and relativistic terms. Was sin not just a breaking of manmade rules and social conventions? After all, didn't the rules of right and wrong depend on the society and culture you belonged to? In a poem published in 1980, I had written, 'If the law accuses me, / hasn't it been invented by people. / If my heart troubles me, hasn't it been formed by words?'[1] For many years I had thought of sin in these naturalistic terms.

To see sin as the mere breaking of man-made rules is also to see it in relativistic terms. It's easy to say to yourself, 'O, they did things that way in such and such a society and in another way in another society. One society believes in polygamy, another in monogamy. Everything is a matter of custom.' It's easy to suppose and believe that everything arose from natural processes and evolution over billions of years, and that human societies are merely part of that process. Nothing is easier than to see sin as another name for the breaking of rules created by man. And nothing could be further from the truth.

The other possibility is that a Being of supreme intelligence and goodness created the universe in the first place. As we have seen, and as we shall see, there are good reasons for believing that such is the case.

Different ways of reading the Bible

Philosopher and theologian Keith Ward says, 'modern scientific knowledge of the universe suggests the idea of a creator with almost compelling force.'[2] For me, no one reconciles the Bible and the beliefs of Christianity with science as satisfyingly as Ward does. He says that what the Bible provides 'is a sacred cosmology, a spiritual interpretation of the universe's origin, nature and destiny, not a scientific cosmology.'[3] The Bible was never meant to be a scientific textbook.

It is wrong to read the Bible literally, as if it were an empirical treatise. The two creation stories in Genesis are placed there side by side 'because they express different, important, spiritual truths.' Literally, the stories are 'incompatible': for example, in the first story (Genesis 1: 1–23) humans are created after vegetation, fish, birds and animals while in the second story (Genesis 2: 4–25) a human male is first created. This is not a worry for Ward. The two stories are 'like metaphors, they cannot contradict one another – only literal accounts can be contradictory – but they may very well complement one another.'[4]

What Ward says here is, I think, hugely important for how we look on the 'truth' contained in the Bible. The Bible is not the literal truth of the scientist and neither is it the propositional 'truth' of the philosopher. God is more subtle than either the scientist or the philosopher. Both the Fundamentalist, who reads the Scriptures literally, and the critic who thinks he finds contradictions in the Bible should pause and consider what the 'truth' given in the Bible really is. It is a truth which is given in words and yet which is beyond words, just as the natural world *points* to the sacred Origin beyond and within itself, so the Bible points to the sacred Being of which the Logos, the Word, the cosmic Christ, is an expression, and there is also the Spirit. As Ward expresses it: 'The Word is the finite image of infinity, embodied in the physical universe through the action of the Spirit, which prepares the way, realises the pattern, guides to the goal, and so expresses the eternal Word creatively in time.'[5]

So God has a threefold nature. The first is 'the unoriginated source of all being, beyond name and form', and this original source is always 'transcendent to every finite reality.' Secondly, there is 'the self-expression of that One in a particular name and form', called variously Logos, the Word of God, the Son of the Father, Wisdom or Christ. Thirdly, there is the Spirit which 'stirs the deep ocean of potency at the beginning of the creation of his space-time.'[6] Ward sums up his discussion of the Trinity: 'This is the threefold face of God: the measureless source of all; its primal self-determination, the Supreme Self, pattern and goal of creation; and the dynamic Spirit of Life, embodying that pattern and realising that goal in the temporal universe.'[7]

Ward's vision of Biblical truth is instructive. Yet we have to be careful too. 'The Word became flesh and made his dwelling with us' according to John 1:14 is a propositional statement based on something that happened in time and in history. There is what might be called literal truth in the Bible in addition to figurative and poetic truth. The God outside of time can speak and reveal himself in history.

Sin and the Fall

In this section, I started off by talking about sin. How does this all link to sin? How does our story – Margaret's and mine – link to the word sin? 'Sin', of course, is a loaded word. It's unfashionable to talk about sin, but whatever terms we use to describe our alienation from the source of Being, it comes to the same thing. It means our life is out of sync. We are transgressing God's known will and as a result are estranged from him. As I explained earlier, I never seriously thought about sin in that way. It was a mere breaking of rules made by humans. As long as one didn't hurt another person deliberately, one couldn't be blamed for anything.

It was only when sin almost broke up our marriage that I gradually came to realise the enormity of being estranged from God. But it took a series of what appeared to us to be miraculous events to finally convince me that such was the case. Margaret's dream had brought us together and she had been told by a Christian who had had a similar experience that the dream was from God. I had accepted that possibility, but when we married, although I thought of myself as a Christian, and despite the dream, I still continued to do things which I knew were wrong. I was going against the light, the light of my conscience and the light of my awareness of God. I wasn't walking in complete obedience to him. Not only that, but if Margaret had truly been sent by God to me as his messenger, as it were, then I should treat her with due love and respect. Perhaps I fell short of recognising who and what she truly was.

The events which took place would finally convince me that there is an actual reality called God, and not just a subjective being or a product of our mind. I would be finally convinced that this Being wishes us to live in accordance with his laws, not just because they are an expression of his nature but because keeping to His way will ensure our happiness as human beings. He wants us to be partners with him in achieving a happier and better world. It had taken me a long time to reach this position. I had been full of sceptical doubts, as my earlier poetry proves, and it took many spiritual trials and sufferings to bring me to the point of true faith. I was a stubborn pupil!

But to understand the enormity of the human estrangement from God, we have to understand the Fall and believe that such is really the case. This is not easy. I remember teaching in the Religious Education class in Gairloch and part of that experience was responding to the scepticism of the pupils regarding Adam and Eve. They appeared to be light-heartedly treating them with disbelief, if not a little amusement. Who were they? When did they live? Wasn't it all just a story or defective history? I probably wasn't equipped at the time to answer their sceptical questions? These, the heirs of the literal interpretation of Genesis.

If I was teaching them now, what I would tell them would probably be along the following lines. It is not history, it is not mere fiction. It is a story with a deep spiritual truth. Adam is representative of what happened at a certain stage in the evolution of the human race. He, she, they somewhere, some time, became aware of the possibility of a Creator and their relationship with him. At the same time they became aware of the possibility of good and evil and of the choice they could make between one and the other.

If, at the time, I had been familiar with the work of the Herman Dooyeweeerd, who I mentioned earlier, I would have been better able to explain to pupils what the Fall actually means. Dooyeweerd's philosophy is profound, all-encompassing and subtle. Dr J. Glenn Friesen, a scholar and interpreter of Dooyeweerd, describes what the fall is in Dooyeweerdean terms:

> The fall must be interpreted as a fall in the religious root of temporal reality; there was a falling away of the heart from its Creator. That is the cause of spiritual death. This spiritual death cannot be confused with bodily death or with eternal death. The acknowledgement of spiritual death as the consequence of the fall is so central that if it is denied, no single part of Dooyeweerd's philosophy can be understood. The fall was in the supratemporal root, which was still an undifferentiated unity. In religious fullness of meaning there is only one law of God, just as there is only one sin against God, and only one mankind that has sinned in Adam.[8]

Man was created as a being in time but still connected to the eternal, to God, through the 'supratemporal root' which the Bible calls the heart and which can either be in a state of apostasy, a turning away from God, or in a state of turning towards him. In the fall man failed in the tasks God had set him, namely, 'to unfold the powers that God had placed in temporal reality' and 'to help redeem the temporal world.' And because man failed, 'Christ's incarnation was required as the new religious root.'[9]

The story is told as a creation story in Genesis, chapter 2. As Ward points out, this second creation story uses 'narrative symbolism' to convey 'spiritual truths.' Humans are formed 'from the dust of the ground.' Matter is given the 'breath of life' by God and the human body is 'fitted for mediating the Spirit of God within the material world.'[10] Humanity is in a place of delight, the garden of Eden, and is in total dependence on God. Adam is commissioned to care for the garden and to build a community of love. For 'wisdom directed by love is self-renouncing, and it allows God alone to rule.'

> Wisdom is symbolised by the 'tree of the knowledge of good and evil', which stood in the garden and which God prohibited until Adam had fully matured in the love of God. When the serpent, another representation of the dragon of chaos, urged humans to

'eat the forbidden fruit', to claim autonomy, knowledge and power, humanity brought destruction upon itself by claiming knowledge without love and without responsibility, in the name of selfish desire. The result would be 'ejection from the garden', loss of the sense of the presence of God, and a slow but inevitable spiritual death.[11]

That is a powerful portrayal of the Fall and its consequences. I am particularly struck by the phrase 'loss of the sense of the presence of God.' For I have felt this myself. One can only feel the loss of something if you have once possessed it, and in the last few years I have come increasingly to feel the presence of God in external nature and in my heart. I now realise how dark and ignorant I was for so many years. But when you are in the darkness, you don't realise that there is such a thing as light. It is only when the light shines that you realise what you have been missing. And you realise that it is the 'wisdom without love', or to use the old term 'sin', which was keeping God from me.

Ward talks about how God gave Adam 'a helper and a partner' and how to be human is to be in relationship with others and how Adam's relationship with Eve was to be one of 'unbreakable relationship and trust.' Trust is a key to a good relationship. Lack of trust caused Margaret and me problems for a time and the suffering it brought us (for we really didn't want to break up) made me realise the link between sin and lack of trust. But, more importantly, the events which happened also brought home to me in a big way my broken relationship with God. And yet that if I trusted him that He was faithful and just.

The serpent's first words to Eve were, 'Did God really say, "You must not eat from any tree in the garden"?' In other words, doubt, lack of trust in God is central to understanding the Fall. Humans became aware of a choice between good and evil. They became agents capable of choice and, therefore, conscious agents capable of trusting or not trusting, of believing or not believing. It was a phase transition from a state of innocence to a state of new awareness and capacity.

From a human, evolutionary point of view, a new being had appeared on the scene with original emergent properties. Its organ of consciousness, the brain, with its radical new abilities, was able to know good from evil and even be aware of its creator. It was what the earth was waiting for, what the universe was being prepared for – beings with the capacity to know and worship the Creator. And, eventually, even this radical thought might appear in that brain when communing with itself about itself: the consciousness I have is not the mere product of a physical, naturalistic process. Rather, I am like a radio receiver which is enabled to receive, as it were, signals from a greater consciousness, a consciousness so great that it is the basis and background of everything.

I had previously thought of all the ways in which Transcendence shines through and reveals itself in the world, the miracle of creation itself, synchronistic events, intuitions, beauty in nature and supernatural happenings. But what I hadn't bargained for was that God could, apparently, reveal himself personally to people and act decisively in their lives; that the infinite could or would bother with mere mortal human beings. If someone had told me twenty years ago, or even ten years ago, that what I am going to recount could happen to anyone, I would have laughed in their face.

There is, of course, a problem and a worry with claims by anyone that God intervenes in human affairs. The problem is highlighted by asking the question, If there is such a God, why didn't he intervene in Auschwitz? For me, there is no rational answer to that question. If God were a good human personality writ large, surely he / she would have prevented Auschwitz. What is clear from Auschwitz and similar atrocities is that man has the freedom to create hell, or heaven, on earth. Take away that freedom and he is no longer human. Speaking humanly, the only way we *can* speak, perhaps the Transcendent, permits human freedom in order to leave us human. But there isn't really an answer to human suffering, only a cry for help. And a faith that despite the appearances of Nothingness, as in Auschwitz, we are not alone.

For despite intense evil, a desire to destroy, there is also an intense good, a desire to create and to uphold. We feel this good in the world and in ourselves alongside the evil. Faith tells us that the good will finally triumph.

Faith happens at a personal level and ours is a personal story. It is utterly trivial in the great scheme of things. Compared to other people's suffering, it is nothing. Yet, we have thought it worth telling. Why?

I suppose because it appears to confirm that, despite appearances, there is something other than naturalism at work in the world. The supernatural events described in the following chapters happened. We were not looking for them to happen. In fact, they were a shock when they happened.

However such events are interpreted, that they happened at all is surely worth telling. Whatever their interpretation, they appear to contradict scientific naturalism. They point strongly to a supernatural element in the world. For that reason alone we thought they were worth recording.

• 13 •
Annus mirabilis – (1)

A lack of trust

In retrospect we can look back on the year in which the following events took place as our annus mirabilis, although at the time it was sometimes more like our annus horribilis (as Queen Elizabeth II named the year 1992). The horrible part was our lack of trust in each other and the amazing, even miraculous, part was what we took to be the intervention of the transcendent. The lack of trust stemmed from what I will refer to as 'my sins' and 'her sins.' The intervention of the transcendent I will attribute to the reality that Christians call God.

So far, I have spoken at length about how my beliefs regarding existence and the world were changing. I became more and more open to the possibility of a supernatural reality which impinges in many ways on the temporal realm. Many of the factors which made me change my mind are open to scientific scrutiny, such as the creation event and the information systems of DNA. Other things, such as intuitions of the divine and beauty in nature may not be susceptible to scientific analysis but they are widespread, and potentially universal, among human beings.

But what finally convinced me of the existence of a divine Source external to ourselves were sequences of objective incidents in my life and Margaret's which cannot be explained rationally: that and the inner transformation which I felt was taking place in me, which can only be felt by the person experiencing it and is, therefore, difficult to communicate. Christians call this the work of the Holy Spirit. Millions of people have attested to this work in the inner self over the centuries.

What can be told are the external supernatural incidents. These on their own don't prove the existence of a deity. But they do point to a supernatural side to the world that makes the existence of a mind beyond the physical more likely.

My account, and Margaret's, of what happened has to be taken on trust, just as the most important things in the world and in life have to taken on trust. What happened to us makes me realise that *trust* is of fundamental importance and permeates all relationships and human interactions and transactions. Human society couldn't survive without it. Trust is equally important in our relationship with the divine. But, of course, we have to believe God exists before we can begin to trust in him!

I retired from teaching in 2004 aged sixty and retired to Staffin where I was born and where my father had been a Free Church lay preacher all those many years ago. 'Retirement' for me was a misnomer. I was happily kept busy with various writing projects for schools and for the Gaelic College in Skye. I liked nothing better than to be busy. Margaret worked in a local nursing home for a couple of years. Our marriage wasn't perfect, but then, which marriage is. As a result of the Fall we are flawed like everyone else.

But we continued to believe in God and that he had brought us together through Margaret's dream. Our real suffering started some time after we came to live in Staffin. The trust we had in each other started to evaporate. We would argue and there would be a dreadful atmosphere between us. This would sometimes last for days. Then things would get better and we would be friends again. This was to be the pattern of our lives for almost two years. Suspicion, mistrust, arguments and then reconciliation. This was repeated and repeated month after month. Many a time we almost broke up, but something prevented it, something that was more powerful than either of us.

Then we started going to the Free Church in Staffin where the Rev. John MacLean was the minister. In the first or second service we attended, some of the verses chosen for the singing were Psalm 37, 3–5: Set thou thy trust upon the Lord, / and be thou doing good; / And so thou in the land shall dwell, / and verily have food. Delight thyself in God; he'll give / thine heart's desire to thee. / Thy way to God commit, him trust, / it bring to pass shall he. Little did the Rev. MacLean know that these were the verses my late father had written down on a piece of paper and given to me some forty years previously. The Lord had given my father these verses for me. It was the one and only time he had ever given verses to me. My mother, bless her, was always getting verses from the Lord for me and gently prompting me to follow Christ, but for my father it was a one off.

The first and second fall of the stick

Shortly after this, on the 21st of July of that year, something happened which would in the end completely change the course of events. I have already mentioned that Margaret had started writing a book about her life. Since we got married, the subject would be mentioned from time to time. The dream and all that had happened to us seemed to be something worth telling. We had spoken of writing the book together, but this would be put on hold, either through pressure of other work or our arguments.

On the weekend of the 19–20th we had a visitor, a lady from Canada who was doing some sociological and Gaelic research in Scotland. We told her our story, how we had met, the dream and how we had married and she thought it was something that was well worth telling.

The next day, on Monday 21st July at about 5pm, our usual dinner-time, we were sitting at the table in the kitchen-dinette when Margaret said to me, 'Maybe we *should* write the book.' Just then there was a clatter outside the door leading into the hall. I went out to investigate and was surprised, not to say a little bit alarmed, that the stick for opening the loft had fallen off its hook and was lying on the floor. I had been sixteen years in the house and nothing like it had ever happened. In fact, supernatural kinetic activity of any kind had never happened in our lives up till then. The stick is 12 mm square, 75cm long, weighs 80 grams. There is a hook screwed into the wood at one end for hanging on to a nail in the wall. The other end has a plastic device for fitting into the latch of the door to the loft. The stick hangs perpendicularly and is reasonably heavy, which ensures that it cannot dislodge from the hook on its own.

We were stunned that this had happened. I was much more stunned than Margaret as I probably have a more vivid imagination and all kinds of thoughts were racing through my head. To me it was a supernatural event. Sticks just don't fly off hooks on their own. There has to be a cause such as wind or a disturbance of some kind. There was nothing physical I could think of to make that stick fall.

I have already mentioned the Gaelic word *manadh* and how when I was teaching Gaelic in Gairloch I had come across stories involving *manaidhean* (plural). It can mean 'omen, sign, apparition.' In the old days in the Scottish Highlands such omens were not uncommon. I remembered reading that when pieces of wood – perhaps lying on the floor or loose floor-boards – rattled together that it could be the premonition of a death. The wood was needed for making the coffin. Other manadh could be aural. One story was of loud noises heard in a church, followed by a funeral.

The fall of the stick, therefore, worried me, as I thought it might be a *manadh*. At the time, I didn't connect it with the writing of this book, although Margaret at the time suggested that there might be some connection, because we were talking of writing the book at the very moment when the stick fell.

Be that as it may, a week later, on the following Monday we had gone to bed and were falling asleep when we heard a clatter. I went to investigate. The stick was lying on the floor again. If anything, this alarmed me more than the first time. For the stick to come off the hook on its own once with no-one near it was bad enough, for it to happen a second time reinforced the feeling that 'someone' was trying to tell us something. But what?

I start to clear the loft

The loft is a big one and runs the length of the house. The longest part of it is to the left as you enter it via the ladder, and that part was full of packing boxes filled with books and papers. The shorter section to the left was also full of boxes filled with books, folders and papers, the legacy of a lifelong passion for reading. There had never been enough room in my small study for all the books and papers I had accumulated and Margaret did not want another bookcase in the living room! I decided to clear the loft of most of the boxes. If anything was going to happen to me, I didn't want to leave it to others to clear up after me. Also Margaret was afraid of clearing lofts as she had previously fallen through a loft and suffered two cracked ribs.

Reluctantly, for the next two weeks I was clearing our loft. I started on the longer section and made good progress. Some boxes of papers I burned. Others I took to the main dump for the area in Portree, some 20 miles away. By the 14th of August, I had cleared a substantial number of boxes but there were a few at the far end of the shorter section which I still had to check. I didn't throw all the books out. I was hoping that I would live for a few years yet and that some of the books which I valued would still be of use to me!

While all this was going on, we had planned a four-day coach holiday in the Cotswolds from the 15th to the 18th. However, after booking the holiday we were arguing and I decided, unilaterally, on the 13th to cancel the holiday. Margaret, naturally, was not pleased. She felt she was in a prison. The Biblical story of Joseph was important to her. She felt like Joseph in prison. But that was not all. Early on the morning of the 14th, as she woke up, the name 'John Bunyan' came strongly to her mind and also the word 'prison.' She got up and looked on the Internet for information about Bunyan. She was surprised to find that he had been in prison and that he had written *Pilgrim's Progress* in Bedford Jail.

When I got up, I was surprised to see her at the computer so early in the morning and she explained to me what had happened. I found it vaguely interesting that she had thought of John Bunyan who had written *Pilgrim's Progress*. Our pilgrimage, it appeared, wasn't making much progress!

However, there were a few surprises in store. After breakfast that morning I proceeded with clearing the loft. There were three boxes at the far end of the shorter section which I had to check. There were about a dozen books in one of the boxes. I picked one up. It was a Gaelic version of the *Pilgrim's Progress* that had belonged to my father many years before and that had somehow come into my possession. I had no idea that I had such a book. It had apparently been given to my father by a Free Church minister, whose name was on the inside page. I came down from the loft and said to Margaret, 'This book might be for you.' I told her how I had found it in the box I had chosen to clear.

She was surprised, to say the least. She started reading the book, but she finds English easier to read and when she was visiting a friend one or two days later she asked her if she had a copy of the *Pilgrim's Progress* in English. Her friend said, 'Yes, in fact, I've been tidying the spare room and I came across a copy.' She gave her the *Pilgrim's Progress* and Margaret read it. It is, of course, a Christian classic and tells the story of Christian's and his wife Christiana's trials on the road to the celestial city. Many a pit of despair they encountered but they entered in by the narrow and difficult gate and in the end they were triumphant.

The 'gate' in Margaret's dream

It was, of course, a gate Margaret had seen in the dream. She had seen me in front of her and had followed me through the gate. It was about this time that it suddenly dawned on me what the gate in Margaret's dream really represented. The gate was not merely a gate pointing her towards me, perhaps meeting me or even marrying me. No, the dream and the gate represented something far more profound and important. It was Christ, the gate, him, the gateway to eternal life, portrayed so brilliantly in Bunyan's book. It is a gate not easily entered as I was beginning to find out. A narrow gate as it says in the Bible and few there are that enter. This may seem to fly in the face of modern democratic principles. On the other hand to strive, suffer and endure may mean gaining something worthwhile in the end. The Apostle Paul describes the Christian life as a race and this symbolism will be readily understood by contemporary sensibilities where the race and competition is part of the culture. The winner is applauded for trying. Of course, the other side of the coin is that salvation is a free gift. We don't win it by our efforts: God gives freely by his grace.

On the morning of the 14th, after I had given Margaret the copy of the *Pilgrim's Progress*, I made my way with more boxes to the dump. On my return, about 1pm, I noticed a car at the door. Who was it but the Rev. MacLean. I was surprised, as he hadn't been to the house before. Margaret, perhaps, attached more significance to his visit than I did. After the fall of the stick, and the Bunyan incident in the morning, it was a notable event for the minister – a 'man of God' – to appear.

After chatting back and forth, I enquired what had sent him our way. He explained that he had been looking in the phone book for another number and that our number kept cropping up and that he was, as it were, prompted to visit us. At the back of my mind, I thought, 'Well, maybe it's because we have started going to his church.' Nevertheless, it was rather strange that he had come on that precise day and was 'prompted' by the Spirit to come.

I told him about the stick incident and some of the things that had happened to us and asked him if he had heard of anything supernatural of the kind happening to anyone else. He hadn't heard of anything such as had happened to us, although he did recall some strange and apparently supernatural events that he had come across in his ministry. The sound of a baby crying although there was no baby there. The appearance of an 'angel' at a time of crisis. At least, it comforted me that he didn't just write off what had happened to us as nonsensical. God could use many means to bring people to Himself.

What happened with the fall of the stick probably had more effect on me than on Margaret. This was because I had been sceptical about the supernatural. It was always something that happened to other people. And while I could believe that poltergeist activity did happen, from the accounts I had read of such activities they did not seem to have purpose or specific meaning. What had happened to us appeared to be both specific and to have purpose. For example, finding the *Pilgrim's Progress* on that specific day and the sequence of events leading up to me finding the book.

Looking over the events of our lives as we have described them, there seemed to me to be a remarkable pattern emerging which could only be explained by the guiding of a superior, yes, even a supernatural and all-knowing, power.

• 14 •

Annus mirabilis – (2)

A strange dream and a broken car

A few weeks before the stick incident, I had a rather strange dream. There were three very white rectangles, like signs, appeared in front of me. On the middle one in black letters was the word 'death', on the one to the left there were three letters which I took to be the end letters of someone's Christian name and the one to the right was blank. I was rather puzzled and a little alarmed. It was seldom I remembered my dreams, but this dream made an impression on me. It was partly the peculiarly bright whiteness of the signs.

Within the week I had been to two funerals. Both people had been ill and their deaths were not unexpected. As it so happened, the three letters which I had seen on the sign in the dream were an abbreviation of one person's full Christian name. I thought to myself, 'Well, there were three signs. Did that mean there would be three deaths?' Frankly, I was worried that it might be my own.

I drove the fifty miles to the Gaelic College in Skye three days a week. A few days after the dream I was driving south and approaching a series of sharp bends where the road snakes round the Cuillin Hills at a place called Druim na Cleòc. Before I came to the first bend, there came a flash to my mind's eye of the dream and the brilliantly white signs. As I came round the second bend the car went out of control as if the steering had gone and I struggled to keep it on the road. It crossed the double white line to the other side. Eventually, as it slowed down, I was able to control it. I breathed a huge sigh of relief. There could easily have been a vehicle coming towards me at what was a busy time of year and a busy time of day. I thanked God that I hadn't crashed.

But that wasn't quite the end of the matter. I drove slowly to a nearby parking place and phoned Margaret who got in touch with a local garage. They came eventually with the breakdown lorry and took the car to the garage. Not only that, but they gave me a lift to the Gaelic College and they said they would examine the steering and let me know the outcome. Later that day they phoned and said they could find nothing wrong with the steering and that it was okay to drive the car. That evening my daughter-in-law, who lives near the College, gave me a lift to the garage where I picked up my car and drove the fifty miles home to Staffin. Because of the fright I had earlier, I drove reasonably slowly. Perhaps just as well!

As I approached our home in Staffin, just at the road-end above our house, the gears packed in and it was stuck in 3rd. I negotiated the last few hundred yards in 3rd but the car refused to go up the steep gradient to our house and I left it there, one hundred yards from home. I thanked the Lord for the day's events and that he had taken me safely home. The reason I had lost control on the bend was that the gears weren't working properly. The only hint I had had of something wrong with them was that it had been sometimes difficult to get it into gear. Apparently, as I was told later by a mechanic, if you are going reasonably fast round a bend and the gears aren't synchronising, it can mean loss of control. I had to get a new gearbox and the steering has been fine since.

What struck me about all this was that the dream I had seemed to be warning me of danger. Not precisely what the danger was, but still a warning. If I had been more aware of the promptings of what the 'greater self', God, or whatever, was giving me and the information I was getting, and more sensitive to what was going on, for example, when the flashback to the dream came just before the bend in the road, I might have slowed down. I hope it taught me the lesson to be sensitive to what the spirit is telling me.

There was only a probability that there would be a collision. All this led me to the thought that the future is probabilistic. Events leave room for human freedom. That day I could have died as easily as lived. What would happen depended on a multiplicity of decisions by others. For example, what time such-and-such vehicle would leave Kyle or some other place. Would it be at the precise spot when I crossed the double white line? No doubt the All-knowing knows what is going to happen and (allowing for anthropomorphic-speak) can control events, though not within the constraints of a mechanistic, Newtonian universe.

The stick falls a third and fourth time

While working at the College, I continued in a sporadic way to write this book. There was pressure of other work but, more pertinently, arguments arising between Margaret and me from lack of trust. Things would go well for a while and then there would be a domestic explosion. This would mean I couldn't get on with the book. What was the point of writing our story if the end result was two bickering Christians? If our theory was correct that God had brought us together and if indeed he wanted us to write the book, for whatever reason, the journey to the completion of the said book was indeed a hard one.

Even now as I write, a year later, I have no idea when or how the book will be finished. But I feel it must be finished, even if, because of lack of trust, our relationship as man and wife were to fail. I have two main reasons for this: firstly, I wish to make clear how my beliefs have changed from scepticism and a belief in naturalism to a firm belief in God and, secondly, I wish to record how what has happened to Margaret and me has confirmed these beliefs in a remarkable way. When I consider all that has happened, I am lost in amazement and continually give thanks to God for his mercy. Supposing there was only this life, still I am grateful for the glimpses I have seen of the glory of the Being behind all things.

More remains to be told of things that have happened while writing this book. Time has passed. It is a year last July since the stick first fell. The fall of the stick no longer frightens me as it did when it first fell. The reason for this is because I believe the stick falls for a reason. It has fallen on a further three occasions this year and every time I have felt there is clear reason behind its falling. Twice the stick has been telling us, 'Stop your arguing and get on with the book.' Once the fall of the stick seemed to know what Margaret was thinking. It had a message for her. What has happened with the stick, Margaret's dream and other events in our lives forces me to think of this possibility: that there is an All-knowing, intelligent agency which wills people to do good; that this agency is interested in people, their lives and relationships; and that this agency wishes people to have a relationship with it based on mutual trust. People call this force for good God.

The stick fell a third time. It was not that we were waiting for it to fall. Far from it. It was something quite outside our volition. All I know is that it fell without anyone near it and this has had an effect on how I view reality.

I had written quite a lot of the book by then and it wasn't what Margaret had envisaged. As the reader who has read thus far will know, I have written much about my intellectual struggle with faith. For Margaret, a lot of it seemed to be dry and academic and she was afraid that people would be put off by this more intellectual content, where I was using references to texts and so on. On the other hand, I thought it was important to tell the story of a person's striving to understand what the world was all about and one's trying to find out what was true and not true.

On that morning Margaret had been having a struggle in her mind with the type of book it would be. She was in the hallway putting the Hoover back in the cupboard, a few feet away from where the stick hung on its hook. I was in my study at the computer and could hear her doing this. Suddenly, the stick jumped of its hook and landed on the floor about three feet away from her. I heard her call. I came out and she explained what had happened. I could see it all for myself. The stick had come off the hook and was lying on the floor.

Rightly or wrongly, Margaret took this to mean that she was being warned that she was wrong in her thinking regarding the type of book it would be; that it should be written precisely as it was being written. I carried on writing.

The fourth time the stick fell was even more outrageous *in naturalistic terms*. Not outrageous at all of course if one believes in supernatural agency. By this time, personally, I was convinced of the intervention of supernatural agents, or a supernatural agent, in our lives. The world of a scientific viewpoint which only believes in determinate *physical* cause and effect was being left far behind. What was happening to us could not be explained in these simplistic terms.

I had been away from home teaching a summer Short Course in the Gaelic College for a week. Margaret and I had been getting on well for a few weeks and I had made up my mind to get on with 'the book' on my return. On the Friday, after coming home, we started to argue. The argument became more heated and to avoid further hassle I picked up some bedding, a towel and toilet bag and went to sleep in my sister's house next door. Her house was empty at the time and I slept in the upstairs bedroom.

I awoke about 2am and had been dreaming. In the dream there was the black ash left by a fire and someone, a woman, I'm not sure who, was searching in the ashes of the past. I was going back to sleep when I heard a loud knocking outside. I went to the window. The outside door was below the upper bedroom window and I could see that it was Margaret at the door. 'Yes,' I said, 'what's the matter?' 'The loft is falling down,' she replied, and off she went without any further explanation. The remark intrigued me and I thought I had better investigate. I dressed quickly and went up to our house.

What I found staggered me. The door to the loft was lying on the floor with the stick beside it. The stick had come off its hook and the hook was still on the nail. The door, which is 24" x 14", has two hinges at one end and a catch at the other. When the catch is turned with the plastic key at the end of the stick, it allows the door to drop down on its hinges. The door had never dropped off its hinges even when hanging open. With the door shut and the catch in place, I thought it highly unlikely that it could have fallen on its own. But not only had the door fallen, so had the stick, and this time it had left the hook on the nail. Afterwards, I regretted not noting whether the latch was in the locked position as it lay on the floor. Not that I suspected Margaret of opening the loft door. If a stick could fall on its own with no-one near it, why not a loft door?

It was obvious that Margaret had got a fright. She told me that she had been late going to bed. She was in the bedroom in her pyjamas and had just got into bed when she heard a sound like a rushing wind and then a clatter. She got up to investigate and was appalled to see the door of the loft on the floor as if it had been wrenched from its hinges and the stick lying beside it. She got dressed quickly and went to tell me what had happened.

Strangely, what happened didn't frighten me at all. I was sure that it was a continuation of what had gone before. Someone or something was telling us to stop arguing and get on with 'the book.' And that is what happened. For a few weeks all was well and I carried on even more urgently writing the book. It became more necessary than ever for me to try and finish it. I was now ready to start on Chapter 13. In a very real sense it was the most difficult chapter to write, together with this one, for I was, and am, describing the relationship between Margaret and me. And that relationship at the time was one of mistrust. I was hoping that it could become once again a relationship of trust and that I could finish the book on that note. Perhaps it will happen by the time 'the book' is written. I hope and trust it will. The important thing for me now is that I trust and believe in God. With Him all things are possible.

The fifth and last time the stick fell

There is, however, one more episode of the stick falling which I have to relate. As before, it involved our falling out. A disagreement started with us on the 8th October and continued for twelve days. On the twelfth day, which was a Friday, it would have been normal for Margaret to go shopping in Portree in the morning. This day I said I would do the shopping in the afternoon and so she stayed at home. She was in the kitchen and I was working as usual at the computer in my study. Suddenly, I heard a cry from the kitchen. The tone of voice made me immediately go and investigate; it was as if something was seriously wrong.

Margaret was in the kitchen in the process of making a cup of coffee when she heard the stick fall. This time she was deeply shaken. She was shivering and she started to cry and couldn't stop. Perhaps at long last the wounds of mistrust would begin to heal. Shortly afterwards, when she had recovered her composure, we were in the sitting room. I took the Bible and opened it at random and put my finger on a verse. I said, 'This verse is for you.'

The verse was Esther 1:22 – 'He sent dispatches to all parts of the kingdom, to each province in its own script and to each people in its own language, proclaiming in each people's tongue that every man should be ruler over his own household.'

If I had known the story behind the verse, I would have laughed there and then. But I wasn't familiar with the story. It was, of course, about Queen Vashti who had humiliated King Xerxes by refusing to come to his banquet. He ruled over 127 provinces stretching from India to Cush and he arranged a great banquet in his royal citadel of Susa for the military leaders and princes and nobles of the provinces. This drunken spree went on for 180 days. Finally, he sent an invitation to bring before him his Queen Vashti so that all the people and nobles could admire her beauty, but she point blank, apparently, refused to come.

And so she was deposed and a decree to that effect was sent throughout the empire. The verse I quoted was part of the king's dispatches. Without going into details of our relationship, this story of Xerxes and Queen Vashti was, in its own way, highly relevant to our case. I hope not relevant in the sense of our relationship ending. But in other ways the story seemed to speak to us.

And so the stick fell for a fifth time. I hope it is the last time, for it appears to me that the fall of the stick is trying to tell us something. And what it has been telling us, apparently, on the last three occasions, is to get our relationship in order and to write this book.

The fall of the stick – and it is important to keep in mind the context in which all this happened – and everything else that has happened to me in the past 20 years has had a major impact on me as a person. It has caused no less than a revolution in my thinking. The person I was then, say 40 or even 20 years ago, and the person I am now appear to be two quite different people. The main difference, I suppose, is that I am now convinced that at the basis of the world is a metaphysical reality whose essence is love.

As a person who has always been interested in philosophy and the progress of science and how these relate to religion, I find it fascinating how these three areas of knowledge have started to coalesce, or, at least overlap in the last 50 years or so. In the 19th and 20th centuries, science and religion seemed to be on a collision course. Human rationality was supreme. Science was seen as revealing the truth about the world through reason and experiment. Religion was seen by many in the West as bronze-age myths waiting to be outgrown. Atheistic modernism spawned philosophies such as Marxism and forms of existentialism declaring the death of God.

At the beginning of the 21st century things are not as clear-cut. Various developments and discoveries, such as the Big Bang theory of the origin of the universe and the amazing complexity revealed in the development and evolution of life, continue to blur the boundaries between science and religion. Now we have physicists sounding like theologians and theologians sounding like physicists. And the philosophers give their own versions of what life might entail, as has always been the case.

• 15 •

Where science and religion converge

The creation event

Earlier I described how in youth science had confirmed to me my unbelief, or, perhaps I should say, my inadequate knowledge of science had done so. Now more than fifty years on, and rather than diminishing my faith, science is playing a part in confirming it. Of course, a living faith is much more than mere intellectual assent. It is a response of the whole person to reality. Theologian Hans Küng affirms, with reference to the doubts raised by the philosophy of Kant, that no 'theoretical proof of reason' will convince us of the existence of God and the self but that this rather comes from a 'practically realised ... fundamental trust,' something that involves the 'whole person.'[1]

As I have tried to show, a whole series of events that I experienced personally brought me to the stage where I can say, 'Yes, God exists and I am certain of it.' Some of these were inner experiences, one could say subjective, and some also were what is called objective, that is, I experienced them as events in the external world. Margaret was a part of many of the latter. A world without God is a world with no absolute guarantee of its reality. There is only turmoil of competing rationalities all stemming from human invention. On the other hand, a world issuing from a transcendent and immanent being of supreme goodness and intelligence guarantees the intelligibility and wisdom of the world.

From a scientific point of view, nothing has more clearly demonstrated that rationality and wisdom than what science has discovered in the past forty or so years. The Apostle Paul could say in Romans 1:20 'For the invisible things of him from the creation of the world are clearly seen, being understood by the things that are made, even his eternal power and Godhead ...' In the Apostle Paul's time science was in its infancy. It had to wait until now to confirm in the most amazing way possible what Paul was saying through faith. Possibly the most awe-inspiring discoveries are those of the cosmologists.

That a creation event – the big bang – took place some 14 billion years ago is now accepted by the 'vast majority of physicists and cosmologists,' according to Dr Francis Collins, head of the Human genome Project (1993–2008). There is now overwhelming positive evidence for such an event, such as the recession of the galaxies, the 'afterglow' radiation from the initial annihilation of matter and antimatter and the 'ratio of certain elements throughout the universe, particularly hydrogen, deuterium, and helium.'[2] In addition, Martin Rees mentions measurements that 'if they had turned out differently' would have refuted the theory. Among these are that the level of helium in objects is not too high and the masses of neutrinos 'seem to be too low to embarrass the theory.'[3]

Although Edwin Hubble published data in 1929 showing that nearby galaxies were receding from our own, it was not until much later that further evidence seemed to prove that the universe had begun at a single point some fourteen billion years previously. Penzias and Wilson, for example, discovered the residual background radiation left over from the big bang in 1965.

As a non-scientist, but as a person with a strong interest in the findings of scientific research of all kinds, I find the big bang scenario astounding, even mind-boggling. It all began in a fireball of incredible density and incredible temperature. Says Martin Rees, 'Only for a few minutes would the temperature have exceeded a billion degrees. After about half a million years it had cooled to 3000 degrees ...'[4] From these incredible few minutes would eventually unfold the stars, the galaxies, the table of elements, and life itself. It is worth pondering that at that moment when time itself began, everything, including our world and life itself was there as potentiality. Our world and our sun were far in the distant future. But everything in that initial phase had to be finely tuned if life or anything like it was eventually to emerge.

It is the fine-tuning which makes this event so unbelievable. In a survey of current thinking on big bang cosmology, philosopher and expert on the Anthropic Principle, John Leslie, describes what is involved in this fine-tuning. It is not one factor that has to be precise beyond human imagining but a whole series of factors. Things such as 'force strengths, particle masses' and 'expansion speed.' Here are just a few examples of the precision involved: for a universe such as we see around us the initial speed of expansion would need to be just right. In 1978 Dicke calculated 'that a decrease of one part in a million when the Big Bang was a second old would have produced recollapse.' And S. W. Hawking 'estimated that even a decrease by one part in a million million when the temperature was 10E + 10 degrees'[5] would have the same result. Rees mentions N the number 1, 000, 000, 000, 000, 000, 000, 000, 000, 000, 000, 000, 000. This number represents the strength of the 'electrical forces that hold atoms together, divided by the force of gravity between them.' This number N is absolutely crucial for the type of universe we inhabit. If it had been only a few zeros less, only 'a short-lived miniature universe' could have evolved. There would not have been enough time for the evolution of life.[6]

I could go on with numerous examples of fine-tuning but they all lead to the question, How could this be? One can believe it all happened by mere chance or quantum fluctuation or that we are part of a multiverse. Or we could believe what it says in Genesis, the words with which the Bible start: 'In the beginning God created the heaven and the earth.' Intuition and imagination help me to decide. I can imagine an eternal and necessary Being of unimaginable power and intelligence saying 'Let there be light.' I can imagine such a Being starting the whole creative process. I cannot imagine it happening on its own, even if time were infinite, so precise the numbers involved and so numerous the necessary refinements.

Dooyeweerd and the findings of science

The creation event, of course, is central to the Christian understanding of the world. Herman Dooyeweerd goes back to the Greek beginnings of Western philosophy and disputes any form of dualism such as the form / matter view of the Greeks, the Nature / Grace dichotomy of the middle ages and the Nature / Freedom idea theory of the Enlightenment. He calls these 'ground motives' in that they influence the way people think and act. They underpin what people think reality is all about.

On the contrary, he believes that all experience, everyone's experience, is religious in character, whether they realise it or not, because God is the origin of all things and we live in a cosmos created by God. The 'ground motive' of Creation, Fall into sin and redemption in Christ is revealed to us in the Bible. It is the ground motive of the Christian and governs the way he or she sees everything. The Fall took place in the human religious root and it meant a spiritual death, a falling away from the 'supratemporal' reality within. It was a falling away from man's true selfhood. Dooyeweerd's philosophical treatment of the human's place in time, the nature of time and its connection with eternity is both thorough and subtle and I can only touch on it here.

Interestingly, when he wrote his New Critique in the 1930s the scientific evidence for a creation event was still in the future. In a marvellous way, the discoveries of the last forty years confirm and add weight to Dooyeweerd's claims. For example, he claims that the initial creation, including the creation of man, took place before cosmic time began. This links in with the claim of even the *weak anthropic principle*, namely that a great number of the fundamental physical constants are within a very narrow range – the only range suitable for the emergence of life. From a human point of view, it would appear that God, before the Big Bang, before time began, in eternity was 'planning' the creation of life and human beings.

Even more remarkable is the convergence of another aspect of Dooyeweerd's thought with the findings of the latest science. For Dooyeweerd, 'Nothing in creation is being or substance; created reality exists only as *meaning*, restlessly *referring* back towards God as *Arché* or *Origin* ... God *expresses* Himself in His creation, and created reality *refers* back to God.'[7] (author's emphasis) Only God has Being and everything comes from him. And there is no substance, only meaning. MIT trained scientist Gerald L. Schroeder says:

> One hundred years ago, no J. A. Wheeler would have dared to suggest that all we see about us is actually the expression of condensed information. He'd have been dismissed as a mystic. But then one hundred years ago who would have dreamt that the solid world is really 99.9999999999999 per-cent empty space made solid by hypothetical, force-carrying, massless particles? And that even that minuscule fraction of matter that is matter

may not actually be matter, but wavelets of energy that we
material beings sense as matter.[8]

If Wheeler and others are correct then 'information may be the
fundamental substrate of our universe.' For Schroeder that means that,
'every particle is an expression of information, of wisdom.' The universe
was created with information as an intrinsic part of it. The consciousness
I have is part of 'cosmic history.' It doesn't arise from the brain 'de novo.'
'Aspects have been present from the start, the very start, the Big Bang.
Consciousness, as wisdom, is as fundamental as existence itself,' says
Schroeder.[9]

Two scientists and the miracle of creation

But to really appreciate how real and important information is, and
therefore meaning, to the reality we inhabit, we have to look to biogenesis,
the origin of life. That is what acclaimed physicist Paul Davies does in his
book *The Fifth Miracle*, sub-titled 'The Search for the Origin of Life.' We
have to treat his title with caution. Although the 'bio-friendly universe'
is for Davies of 'a stunningly ingenious character' he does not appear to
believe in miracles in the supernatural sense. In the preface he has 'no
doubt that the origin of life was not in fact a miracle.'[10] Yet at the end
of his book he does not deny the possibility 'of a self-organizing and
self-complexifying universe, governed by ingenious laws that encourage
matter to evolve towards life and consciousness.' This in contrast to the
view of 'orthodox science, with its nihilistic philosophy of the pointless
universe, of impersonal laws oblivious of ends ....'[11]

What Davies brilliantly describes explains why he is right to have
doubts about 'orthodox science.' The organization of the simplest living
cell is as complex as the organization of a city. There are masses of
'specialized molecules' going hither and thither, all of them doing specific
jobs. And yet there appears to be no 'intelligent supervisor' running the
show. Davies goes on to explain that the complexity of the living cell is
'information-based complexity.'[12] In that sense it is like a book. DNA itself
is like an 'instruction manual' and the atoms have to be in exactly the
right order, although there are millions of them.

Although his scientific background appears to prevent Davies from coming out and saying decisively that the universe is ultimately the product a transcendent intelligence, the language he uses when speaking of life and the organisation of matter has a religious feel to it. We are reminded how close the honest contemporary scientist, the physicist especially, is to the theologian. Davies speaks with awe of the mystery of the origin of life. The odds against it happening by chance are 'mind-numbingly huge.'[13] 'Hundreds of thousands of specialist proteins are needed' for life as we know it. The odds against them appearing by chance are about 10^{40000} to one.[14]

No wonder he uses words like 'mystery', 'miracle', 'fluke, 'self-organising' and 'complexity' throughout *The Fifth Miracle*. I for one am convinced that the 'specific randomness' which is found in biological systems is, as he says, 'a fact of the deepest significance.'[15] My intuition, informed by the information given by scientists like Davies, is that the universe and life is no accident but is the product of an intelligence and power beyond our comprehension.

Davies is to be applauded for the stark honesty of his conclusion. As we have noted, he pits two diametrically opposed world views against each other. The one sees humans as the result of mindless contingent events, the mere nihilistic product of chance alone driven by a pitiless evolution. This is 'orthodox science' and he quotes people like Stephen Jay Gould and Jacques Monad as examples of this view. The other view is

the vision of a self-organising and self-complexifying universe, governed by ingenious laws that encourage matter to evolve towards life and consciousness. A universe in which the emergence of thinking beings is a fundamental and integral part of the overall scheme of things. A universe in which we are not alone.[16]

This is not so far from the vision of the theologian who believes that the universe was created by a wise Creator. Not only the universe, of course, but human beings who could believe in and worship that same Creator.

Science and theology are not so far apart after all. If Schroeder sees the universe as the expression of a transcendent Creator and a singular wisdom, and if Davies suspects that life is not the mere product of chance,

Francis Collins, one of the world's leading geneticists, is a person who has accepted Jesus Christ as his saviour.[17] In a fascinating account, *The Language of God, A Scientist Presents Evidence for Belief*, this gifted and modest man sets forth clearly why he is a Christian believer and why he doesn't see any conflict between science and religion.

He doesn't deny evolution. How could he? The evidence from genetics and the story of DNA alone is overwhelming and detailed. But his faith sits happily with his belief in science. He is as convinced of its reasonableness and value as he is of the reasonableness and value of faith. He is able to square faith with science by his belief in the BioLogos, which is his name for theistic evolution. This Logos, the Word, is the power behind nature and 'to many believers, the Word is synonymous with God.'[18]

His explanation of BioLogos accords with what has been discovered in cosmology and biogenesis. Theistic evolution, or BioLogos, he explains as the creation of the universe from nothingness with the highly improbable fine-tuning of properties needed for life. While the 'precise mechanism' of how life arose initially is unknown, once life took off, evolution and natural selection led over aeons to life as we know it. This happened naturally with no 'supernatural intervention.' Human beings 'are part of this process.' 'But human beings are also unique in ways that defy evolutionary explanation and point to our spiritual nature. This includes the existence of the Moral Law (the knowledge of right and wrong) and the search for God that characterises all human cultures throughout history.'[19]

In other words God created a law-governed universe that allowed life to evolve. God intended to use evolution to bring to being microbes, plants and animals of all kind. He also intentionally used the same method to bring to being creatures with 'intelligence, knowledge of right and wrong, free will, and a desire to seek fellowship with Him.' This all implies a transcendent infinite God outside of space and time who knows all things from the beginning and how they will turn out.

Schroeder and Collins, two scientists with deep knowledge and respect for science but who have in their own different ways a conviction that there is also a spiritual side to reality and a profound belief in a creator God. Another scientist, Paul Davies, who plays with the idea that, cosmically speaking, life might be 'the natural order of things, and that we are not alone.'[20] In other words, the universe is not an accident but was planned.

At the beginning of the third millennium, among open-minded scientists, we can see a convergence between science and religion. I believe this convergence will continue. Religion has no reason to be afraid of science, for if, as I believe, the universe was created by God, what we discover of his creation through science will reinforce belief in him, not destroy it.

But the truth is even more amazing than what either science or theology can encompass in their paradigms, as we shall see.

· 16 ·

What is truth? – (1)

'You are a king then!' said Pilate.

Jesus answered, 'You are right in saying I am a king. In fact, for this reason I was born, and for this I came into the world, to testify to the truth. Everyone on the side of truth listens to me.'

'What is truth?' Pilate asked. (John 18:37–38)

The road has been long and winding. I started off in my young days asking Pilate's question, 'What is truth?' and I said to myself, 'Before I die I want to find out the truth about the world. And if I find out the truth I will write it down one day. And I read and considered and went in by many a door, but like the philosopher in the Rubáiyát I 'Came out by the same door where in I went.' Like Pilate, I didn't wait for the answer. More probably, Pilate thought he knew the answer already, or thought truth was of a different order to what was in front of him.

The truth proved elusive. For me personally it was a long detour. I discovered that truth wasn't to be found in philosophy and nor was it to be found through reason. Language I found to be a trap. It promised much but in the end it was a kaleidoscope of half promises, bright glittering colours that changed as you looked at them. Nowadays, it's the fashion to deny that there is a meta-narrative, a truth that is true for everyone. And even that can be true, relatively speaking, for the truth that is not the meta-narrative is a relative truth; and most of us most of the time live in relative truths.

There are a lot of people with partial truths. 'I like sunbathing,' says John. True as far as it goes but it's not the whole truth about John. Most truths, whether regarding matters of fact and experience or in the realm of ideas, are both consistent and trivial.

But truth is more subtle, more comprehensive, than can be supposed or suggested by language. Language is a set of symbols and, like any symbol, it is only a pointer to the truth. I believe there is a truth about human life, but it can only be pointed to. It is the truth of the whole human being and the whole human being can be understood only with reference to the Origin of the cosmos itself.

Even when we are facing the truth, it can be avoided. We can say we are merely creatures of time. But Dooyeweerd points us in the right direction. Our I-ness, our selfhood, transcends time. There is a oneness to our consciousness, but there are modes or aspects to it as well. These aspects belong to a whole but they are refracted through the prism of cosmic time, just as pure white light is refracted into the different colours of the spectrum when passing through a prism. According to Dooyeweerd the aspects, or modes of consciousness, are: numerical, spatial, kinematic, physical energy, organic life, psychical feeling, analytical-logical, historical, linguistic, social, economic, aesthetic, jural, moral and the mode of faith.

All these modes have their own truth, their own sovereignty and yet they have a unity as well in the human self, in human consciousness. They go back to the creation of the universe, of cosmic time, which has its roots in God and in eternity. Because of the Fall, human beings have lost contact with God, their true root. This can only be revealed to them in the mode of faith. They become part of Christ, the new religious root, and they know him through the supratemporal self. It was necessary for Christ, the new religious root of man, to come into the world to redeem the world, because man had fallen, had spiritually died.

For Dooyeweerd, to understand that we have a supratemporal self is vitally important. It is what connects time with eternity. This happens in the 'heart' – again a vital part of Dooyeweerd's understanding. It is the central part of our I-ness and it can be in a state of looking away from God or be in a process of renewal.

As I have already observed, a lot of what Dooyeweerd says connects with the findings of modern science, for example, the creation event and information-rich nature at all levels from galaxies to the quantum. It also connects with my own personal experiences.

What is truth?

Truth then is more like a sphere – let us say of glass – with a vast number of facets. And at the centre of the sphere is the still, small point of which nothing can be said, the eternal centre. It cannot be spoken of because it is beyond time. All the facets are in time and governed by the laws of cosmic time. They have an analogous connection with each other. When we speak of our life as a race, we are using an analogy. An actual race involves the kinetic – the movement of the limbs; space – the person is moving through space; historical – the race happened in time and it has a history of when it happened; physical energy – the person is using energy; psychical feeling – how the person feels as she runs. The race could involve other aspects also such as the moral – perhaps the race is being run for charity; numerical – the race is timed in the number of minutes it took. Even the mode of faith might enter into it – a person might refuse to run on the Sabbath.

Our reality as humans is through and through analogous. Even the connections between the facets can only be spoken of by analogy. Analogy is a kind of pointing. We humans communicate by language, but language is a very surface phenomenon. It tells us very little about the real world. It is the reason why language is through and through analogous, full of metaphor and simile.

Even an apparently innocent sentence like, 'The cup is on the table' is full of ambiguities. Questions beginning Where? Which? Who? How? What? When? Why? have still to be answered. And even then after we have established where the cup is, on which specific table it is on and who is seeing the cup more questions abound, if we wanted to know the origins of the cup and table. In fact, the questions have only started. How does X see the cup? How do the movements of atoms in her brain enable her to be conscious of the cup? Where did the clay of which the cup is made come from? ... Before long we need to have a cosmos to explain the existence of the cup and table. (Blake's eternity in a grain of sand.) The same applies to anything we can name. It points back to the true Origin.

But analogy becomes even more necessary when speaking of the inner life and feelings. A person might know how you feel if you say you're 'happy' (from Old Norse happ – good luck) but how much more expressive it is to say that you're 'over the moon,' or 'on cloud nine' or 'floating on air.' We use analogies all the time to tell how we feel or what we are thinking, and analogies from different aspects interpenetrate each other.

If this is true of our psychical experiences in the physical world, how much more must it be true of the spiritual? We can point to physical things and, in their cultural context, we can understand what they are and to what use they are put. We cannot point to God in the same way. He is not an object in the 'real' world. In that sense Tillich was right when he said 'God does not exist.' 'Exist' applies to things in time, of which we are a part. God exists 'outside' time in eternity. Even 'outside' is a word of time. Again we are back to analogy.

So how can we know about God? Millions of people claim an experience of God. How can they experience God when he doesn't 'exist'? *We experience God as the ground and origin of all experience.* The still, small invisible point at the centre of all that exists. Everything is in, of and through him. 'For in him we live and move and have our being,'[1] therefore, it *is* possible to experience him. (But remember that even 'him / he' is analogous.) He enables anything and everything to make sense. This is not pantheism, the universe is God, but panentheism – all-in-God. There is a Being pervasive in the cosmos, but who is also separate from the cosmos.

We can only talk with analogies and time-conditioned language such as 'pervasive' and 'separate.' We can only point to God with analogies and metaphors and symbols and such time-conditioned language. But he is yet the most real, for he has enabled the universe to have meaning *from the initial point of creation*, from the centre of the sphere. Without him – a Being beyond time of supreme intelligence, goodness and power – existence would be meaningless.

The Bible is full of analogous language. The Jews more than any other people were aware of the eternity of God, his complete otherness. They are a witness to his works, but they can only point to him in awe as the Being beyond things that exist. But they still speak of him using analogies and poetical language. He is a real presence for them although they cannot physically see him. Here is Isaiah's vision of him in the temple:

> In the year that King Uzziah died, I saw the lord seated on a throne, high and exalted, and the train of his robe filled the temple. Above him were seraphs, each with six wings: With two wings they covered their faces, with two wings they covered their feet, and with two they were flying. And they were calling to one another: 'Holy, holy, holy is the Lord Almighty; the whole earth is full of his glory.' At the sound of their voices the doorposts and thresholds shook and the temple was filled with smoke. 'Woe to me!' I cried. I am ruined! For I am a man of unclean lips, and I live among a people of unclean lips, and my eyes have seen the King, the Lord Almighty.'[2]

This is the language of vision. It may be that physical, supernatural effects accompanied the vision. At one time that would have surprised me, but not now. It reminds one of Otto's language. Isaiah appears to have had a hugely numinous experience of God as the awesome wholly other. He is overwhelmed by what he has experienced. He can only express himself in analogous language.

Open the Old Testament almost at random and one gets a similar use of analogous language. 'He wraps himself in light as with a garment; he stretches out the heavens like a tent ...' (Psalms, 104.2). 'For your Maker is your husband – the Lord Almighty is his name ...' (Isaiah, 54.5). 'Wisdom calls aloud in the street, she raises her voice in the public squares ...' (Proverbs, 1.20).

Reading the Old Testament, it is hard not to come to the conclusion that the Jewish people were in a special relationship with God. Not because the Jews were special – they were no doubt that – but because God chose to reveal himself to them. That is what makes them special for the whole of humanity. Whether it was through supernatural events, like Moses seeing the bush which kept burning, dreams like those Joseph had, God guiding them as a people in a historical setting, or God speaking through his special messengers the prophets; God revealed himself to them. Not a God who could be seen, made with human hands, or a god of myth, but the invisible God who was the origin of all things from nothing.

Christians believe that the revelation continues in Jesus Christ. Humanly speaking, he was also a Jew and his disciples, the propagators of his message, were also Jews. Importantly, this Jesus, who Christians believe was and is the Messiah, the anointed of God, also spoke of God and spiritual matters in analogous terms. But he used analogy and figurative language even more thoroughly than the prophets and poets and law-givers of Israel. As we shall see, it adds powerfully to his claim to be the Christ the anointed of God.

• 17 •

What is truth? – (2)

A personal vision

For me personally it has been a long and tortuous road, a lifelong quest – often mistakenly pursued – an intellectual search, and in the end a revelation, not coming from myself but, I am convinced, from a higher, external, power. Margaret, who was not troubled by intellectual doubts, found my inability to believe mysterious. She finds belief in God a much simpler matter. I envy her and people like her. For me it has always been a narrow gate. But, praise God, he sent her into my life through the dream she had, a dream which cost her many a tear.

From then on, the road has not been straightforward but the end result is stupendous. I feel immensely privileged that the transcendent has entered my life in such a powerful way. Because of the way things have worked out in intimate detail, I cannot but conclude that there is a supernatural all-knowing, loving power behind appearances. That he has entered my life in such a powerful way is truly humbling. For many, God just doesn't speak to people as he did in Old Testament times, through dreams and supernatural events. I beg to differ. I can say 'I beg to differ' because these very things have happened to Margaret and me. It is most strange, but it is true.

The vision I now have of God is of a creator God who created the universe from nothing in a burst of energy that scientists call the Big Bang. Everything was there potentially in the first millisecond, including the creation of man. Gradually, over billions of years, the universe unfolded to what we see today. The universe and our world, including every atom of it, is the sacred expression of this transcendent Being. Before that millisecond, in God's eternally 'existing' mind, the universe to come was imbued with meaning.

By contemplating our own world, the beauty of it, the fine-tuning, how everything fits together so perfectly, we can appreciate its immense sacredness. It becomes impossible to believe that the million synchronisations of 'matter', necessary for life, should just be there by chance. Easier to believe that it comes from an all-knowing centre beyond time. Humans were created in the image of God but have fallen and have died a spiritual death. God speaks to human beings through the heart, the spiritual centre. By believing in Christ, the messenger of God, the Messiah, who is the new spiritual root of mankind, God can communicate with us again and renew us inwardly.

At the end of 2009 when I was on a bus in Edinburgh on a Sunday on the way to church I had a vision of God in my heart. The vision I had of God was of unconditional love. He was a source of heat which sent its warmth out unconditionally to whoever wishes to be warmed. Like a person going into a wood who feels the heat and is aware of a source although she cannot identify it and this source is by necessity good. We destroy ourselves by refusing to be warmed at that fire. God does not destroy us. Let us remember that truth is analogous and that man is fallen. Though the Bible talks of God's wrath and him being a 'consuming fire', we really are ourselves the fire that consumes. We have the power of decision. We can decide to face towards the source of heat or away from it. It is our decision. Christ is the fire which attracts, the presence of God in the world.

This facing towards God or away from him was also a powerful metaphor for me. Looking inwards on my heart I could see that facing towards God was not what I had been doing throughout my life. There was always the lure of sin and it is there always for everyone, if they are honest. The possibility of decision is also there at every instant, of doing good or doing evil. Our choices over time make us what we are.

One cannot face towards God for a minute, or a day, and then look away. Once the belief has been formed, once the light has been lived in, one has to continue to live in the light. And the light – also the heat – can be faint or strong. If it is strong, and you become quite certain God is there and knows every thought of your heart, then you have arrived. God has revealed himself to you. From then on you will live in awe and amazement and joy and wonder for the world which is revealed. And forgiveness will be there, revealed in the act of renewal. As it says, 'But with you there is forgiveness; therefore you are feared' (Psalm, 130.4).

A surprise from Poland

At the end of 2009 a friend who works in Poland suggested I get in touch by e-mail with a Romanian friend of his who was working in Poland. She had an interest in the works of Rudolph Otto. I got in touch with her and she told me how the famous Romanian, Mircea Eliade, an authority on religion, myth and symbol, was influenced by Otto's work. The name Eliade immediately rang a bell with me. This name had appeared to me in a dream 15–20 years previously and at the time I thought he may have been a French poet. For some reason I remembered this name from the dream, although I don't now remember the dream itself. This, in itself, was rather special. Now, through Emilia's e-mail, the name began to mean something for me.

Strangely, I didn't know the work of the scholar Eliade, although he wrote about subjects which interest me. But when Emilia mentioned him in the e-mail, I thought that I must find out more about him and so I purchased his book *The Sacred and the Profane*, which is really a history of the sacred – how the sacred has affected, and appeared in, human societies through the ages. In the introduction he pays homage to Otto's *Das Heilige* (The Sacred) and the extraordinary interest it aroused throughout the world when it was first published. Whereas Otto dealt more with the irrational manifestations of the sacred, Eliade set out to describe the 'sacred in its entirety.'

I ordered the book on the Internet, but before I received it I had decided to have a sacred space to commemorate what had happened to us and to be a focus of worship for the way God had dealt with us. Margaret was a little sceptical about it! Being more traditional, the word 'shrine' was a little bit foreign to her way of thinking. That said, we paid a visit to Inverness on a Saturday before Christmas and I bought a small but elegant table. When we came home that evening the book by Eliade had come by post and was waiting for us. That night, I read it eagerly. It said some very important things to me.

Eliade shows how important the sacredness of a space was for 'religious man' in the past. Nowadays, the sacred has been pushed aside and the

*Top: Staffin in the 1960s. Free Church and Mission House on the left.
Middle: Staffin from Greinigle, early 1990s. Bottom: Staffin Island and
the Torridon Mountains from Flodigarry, Staffin*

A recent photograph of Staffin showing the Free Church and old Mission House (now renovated) on the right, the house where Myles was born

Breasclete, including croft 22 where Margaret grew up

St Kilda, where Margaret was a visiting nurse for a few years in the 1990s

St Kilda, the pier and gable of the old manse

Right: Myles with the bardic crown at the National Mod, 2002

Below: Myles and Margaret at Loch Shianta, Flodigarry with the Dunans in the background

cosmos itself has been 'desacralised.'[1] But it was not always so. When God broke through to speak to humans, that place became holy ground, a sacred place. When God spoke to Moses he said: 'Do not come any closer. Take off your sandals, for the place where you are standing is holy ground' (Exodus, 3.5).

Now what happened to us and what happened to Moses is obviously a facile comparison. It is mentioned here only to illustrate what Eliade meant by a space which becomes sacred. For us the place where the stick fell on its own on five occasions has become a sacred place. The fact that its fall was invested with meaning in the context of our lives is what makes it really sacred, nothing else.

Thus I felt justified in the purchase of the table and I set it up near to the stick with a candle on it to represent the eternal presence of God, a copy of the illustration on the Turin Shroud to represent Christ and a white stone to represent the Holy Spirit. I would have preferred a white dove for this symbol, and the stone will be replaced in due course. Eliade speaks of 'hierophany' – a revealing of the sacred or the divine – and this is what this place represents for us.

The other thing mentioned by Eliade and which left an impression on me was the *axis mundi*. I had seen references to the *axis mundi* in poetry over the years – I think Hugh MacDiarmaid mentions it – but I had never associated it with 'our stick' until I read about it in Eliade's book. It is an idea which entered deeply into the sacred history of ancient tribes, for example, the Australian Achilpa tribe. They took their pole with them on their travels. It was the 'cosmic axis' and if anything happened to the pole, it represented disaster for the tribe. It was the connection for them between the earth and heaven, the realm of the divine. Many other tribes had a conception of the *axis mundi,* and the symbol for the centre of the world, their world, could be a mountain, a ladder, a tree or a pole – an axis, of some kind.

I thought, well, our stick is our *axis mundi*, the means by which the transcendent communicated to us. It is part of the vertical axis. I have sometimes thought of human life and experience in this way, a horizontal axis and a vertical axis. The horizontal axis represents the naturalistic view where things happen in sequence, such as evolution and historical events and the ordinary day to day events in people's lives. All bound in firmly with time and its passage. The vertical axis represents the breaking through of something into time from another dimension, such as the supernatural, or the consciousness of the eternal, or synchronistic events, or a connection with the Origin. The eternal reality is always there but we are only sometimes given awareness of it.

Then, it shouldn't really have been a surprise to me that as I was writing this book on the 4th of January, 2010, and had just started to tell the story about Emilia and Eliade's book, a moving coincidence happened. I had been working on the book for a few hours and had come to the sentence above: '*At the end of 2009 a friend who works in Poland suggested I get in touch by e-mail with a Romanian friend of his who was working in Poland,*' when the postman arrived at the door with a lovely waxed card from Emilia. There was also a postcard with it which had originated in Alba Iulia – where Emilia comes from in Romania – with a painting of the Virgin and child by Gheorge fiul lui Iacov. The waxed triptych card has a beautiful painting of the birth of Jesus. Interestingly, it appears to have a pole like an *axis mundi* pointing towards the infant in the cradle, the first time I had noticed such in a Virgin and child painting.

The postcard has been put in a frame. Margaret happened to have one new unused frame, which she had bought ten years previously, and into which the card fitted perfectly. The golden yellow of the frame was also a perfect match for the paler yellow of the painting. Emilia's framed card has how been placed on our 'shrine', an acknowledgement that, humanly speaking, the divine also contains the feminine.

What is truth? – the end of the road

I have come to the end of my search and I have discovered that the truth is stranger than I could ever have imagined. Some poets, philosophers, scholars and thinkers of various kinds have helped me along the way. But, looking back on my life, unless I am completely deluded, I have all along been guided by a power hugely greater than myself, although I didn't realise it for much of my life. This realization could only come to me after I had come to faith. Now as I look back on my life I see a pattern and, dare I say it, that heaven was merciful to me even when I was a rebel.

What has happened since meeting Margaret has been pivotal. I couldn't have planned any of it. Up until then, I thought that, to some extent, I was controlling my life and what would happen to me. But once I trusted Margaret's dream and that it was from God, and then that we got married, things would never be the same again. Things happened which I had no idea would happen, things I thought that couldn't happen in my wildest dreams did. But if they hadn't happened I would still be stuck in the kingdom of doubt. I can only marvel at the kindness of infinite love.

Only a few years ago, I had strong doubts about the reality of the supernatural. I now have no doubts whatsoever that the supernatural is as real as anything can be, and that is because of what has happened in my own life. And if such things can happen in my insignificant life and, I believe now, in the lives of countless others, how much more so could they have happened in the life of Jesus Christ, who was Emmanuel, that is, 'God with us.' Forget about the horizontal line of evolution and naturalistic explanations. Think of the vertical and how what is outwith time and causality can enter into our lives now.

The events described in the Bible, in the Old and New Testaments, have the ring of truth. They are not mere historical or propositional truths, as philosophers understand truth, but something much more profound. It is the divine revealing itself in human history, the Word becoming flesh. There was Creation by a Creator – the creation of the universe from nothing and the creation of mankind in that first eternal instant. There was the Fall in the religious root of mankind and the turning of man's face from God. And then there was the Redemption of fallen mankind through a stupendous act – the taking on by God the form of man in the person of Jesus Christ.

> Who, being in very nature God,
> did not consider equality with God
> something to be grasped,
> but made himself nothing,
> taking the very nature of a servant,
> being made in human likeness.
> and being found in appearance as a man,
> he humbled himself
> and became obedient to death – even the death on a
> cross!

> Therefore God exalted him to the highest place
> and gave him the name that is above every name,
> that at the name of Jesus every knee should bow,
> in heaven and on earth and under the earth,
> and every tongue confess that Jesus Christ is Lord,
> to the glory of God the Father.[2]

This early creed quoted by Paul clearly expresses the belief in the incarnation of Jesus,[3] that he was 'in very nature God.' This is clearly a great mystery, that the eternal God, the creator of the universe, should empty himself to enter time in human form. And yet that is what the apostles came to believe and that is what is taught in the New Testament. The Jews long expected a saviour sent by God who would 'restore the kingdom to Israel.' Perhaps some thought that a new Israel of a political nature would be established; others that a 'cosmic cataclysm' would herald in a new age.

The 'kingdom' that Jesus heralded was of a radically different kind. Even his closest disciples didn't know what was entailed. When they ask him, 'Who is the greatest in the kingdom of heaven?' he brings a child before him and says that 'whoever humbles himself like this child is the greatest in the kingdom of heaven.'[4] He inverts and subverts all previous values and expectations. When he tells the disciples that he must be killed and on the third day be raised again, Peter objects and says, 'Never Lord! This shall never happen to you!' Jesus tells him he is 'a stumbling-block' and that he does not 'have in mind the things of God, but the things of men.'[5]

Jesus' task was a mighty one. Retrospectively, one can see that only God could have accomplished it. Thinking of it in restricted human terms, it seems impossible. How could one man accomplish the renewal of the human race? Everything seemed against him. He was a poor homeless preacher. His own disciples misunderstood his mission. The clerical establishment was against him. He was given a shameful death outside the city walls. That should have been the end of him. But, contrary to all expectations, he has had more impact than anyone else in the history of the world. Can it be explained?

I don't think it can – in naturalistic terms. It can only be explained as the eternal entering into time. It was a supernatural event of enduring significance. It was the vertical bisecting the horizontal. I would like to look at four elements of Jesus' life in the light of what I have discussed in this book; they are 1) the analogous 2) the numinous 3) prophecies/synchronicities 4) the supernatural elements; the latter especially as it relates to the resurrection.

• 18 •

What is truth? – (3)

Jesus and the analogous

By analogous I mean language used to compare one thing with something else, for example, parables, symbols, metaphors, similes and analogies. Poets deal in figurative language of this kind all the time. It is hugely significant for me that, in this sense, Jesus was a poet through and through. But the poetry is infused with wisdom, beyond ordinary human wisdom. This is what we would expect if he is the wisdom of God incarnate. It is wisdom in the sense of an extraordinary knowledge of the human soul. Much is rightly made of proving the historicity of Jesus and the resurrection. But just as important is the evidence of his words. The high spiritual content contained in the parables, metaphors and sayings all point to a single source: a soul of unparalleled wisdom. It is highly unlikely that the wisdom inherent in his words could have come from different sources.

Of course, Jesus was born into a culture which set a high store on analogous meanings. For the religious Jew the most mundane action or object could be charged with a spiritual meaning. They pointed to eternal realities beyond time. The actions of the Passover at the time of the Exodus are charged with symbolism. The blood of the year-old sheep or goats is to be put on the door-frames. This would mean that the Lord would not destroy the occupants of the houses which had the sign of the blood. For the Passover meal itself, bread made without yeast and bitter herbs were eaten. The bitter herbs were symbolic of their bitter servitude in Egypt while the unleavened bread represented the haste with which they left.

God is always in a relationship with his people as king to subject, as husband to wife, as master to servant, or as father to child. These are always metaphorical pointers and are not of course to be taken literally.

God is a sun, a refuge or living water. The people of God are his bride or a noble vine. There is a rich history in the Bible of looking to God as father and of him treating his people as a father does his children. In his song Moses says: 'Is he not your Father, your Creator, who made you and formed you?'[1] In psalm 65:5 God is called a father to the fatherless, a defender of widows ...' and Isaiah says, '... you, O Lord, are our Father, our Redeemer from of old is your name.'[2]

With Jesus, this metaphor of God as father is carried to an entirely new and unexpected level. If the God-as-father-to-his-people metaphor is strongly professed in the Jewish scriptures, in the Christian New Testament it enters a new phase of development. Now the eternal has entered a human life, Jesus', in a radical manner. He has a special and intense relationship with God as Father, to such an extent that he calls him Abba, an Aramaic word for father implying closeness. In the Gospel of John this relationship reaches sublime heights. The Jews wanted to kill him, not just because he was breaking the Sabbath but because 'he was even calling God his own Father, making himself equal with God.'[3]

But even the disciples are puzzled when he says, 'If you really knew me, you would know my Father as well.' When Philip said, 'Lord, show us the Father and that will be enough for us.' Jesus' reply is instructive:

> Don't you know me Philip, even after I have been among you such
> a long time? Anyone who has seen me has seen the Father. How
> can you say, 'Show us the Father?' Don't you believe that I am in
> the Father, and that the Father is in me? Rather, it is the Father,
> living in me, who is doing the work.[4]

The vision that emerges of Jesus in John is cosmic in its significance. Yes, he is a Jew who is steeped in the symbolic and metaphoric tradition, but he is also something much more. He is God in human form. 'In the beginning was the Word, and the Word was with God, and the Word was God. He was with God in the beginning.'[5] Thus John starts his gospel with these profound and visionary words. And in John, 10:30 Jesus says, 'I and the Father are one.' For saying that, the Jews were ready to stone him. Nowadays, he would be referred to a psychiatrist. But as C. S. Lewis points out, it could only be either a 'lunatic' or God himself who would make such a claim.[6] But, apart from anything else, from the profound psychological insight into human beings that he had, it is clear the Jesus wasn't mad. Mad people do not have the effect on others that he had.

We have already referred to Jesus the poet. His whole way of speaking is permeated with figurative language. One of the key analogies he uses is the 'kingdom of God.' 'The kingdom of God is near. Repent and believe the good news!'[7] But the 'kingdom' is of a radically different kind to what was normally referred to by the word 'kingdom.' Even his disciples would not understand what this 'kingdom' meant until after his death and resurrection. When the Pharisees asked when the kingdom of God would come, Jesus replied, "The kingdom of God does not come with your careful observation, nor will people say, 'Here it is,' or 'There it is,' because the kingdom of God is within you."[8]

Part of his mission was to explain what this kingdom really was. It is like a mustard seed: the smallest of seeds and which grows into a big tree. Or like yeast that is mixed with a large amount of flour to make dough. Or like a net that catches all kinds of fish and the fishermen collect the good fish in baskets but they throw the bad away. Even the spiritual leaders of the Jews were puzzled. Nicodemus, a member of the Jewish ruling council wanted to know about Jesus' 'kingdom' but was mystified when he was told a person had to be born again. He didn't understand that it was a revolutionary inner change that had to take place. 'Flesh gives birth to flesh, but the Spirit gives birth to spirit.'[9]

The birth of the kingdom is mysterious. Jesus compares it to the wind that blows where it pleases. 'You hear its sound, but you cannot tell where it comes from or where it is going. So is everyone born of the Spirit.'[10] It was indeed a radical kingdom. The birth of the kingdom in one is the death of the ego, of the selfish self. It is not being for oneself, it is 'being for others.' Says J. A. Philips, quoting Bonhoeffer, 'being for others' as 'the reversal of all human being' is the experience of transcendence.'[11] Save your life and you will lose it. The seed, the old self, is buried in the ground and the plant from the seed rises towards the light. There is a new creation. The new plant is for the good of others.

So we understand better why Jesus says that, 'You cannot serve God and money.'[12] Acquiring money and being greedy for money is the opposite of 'being for others.'

But how was the kingdom going to be brought to birth? Yes, it was a spiritual kingdom, and it was the individual who was transformed or born again. But how would the kingdom spread in the world and become relevant to the whole human race? This required something other than mere words, great as they were. It required actions, actions which would be a living metaphor, as words were a symbolic metaphor.

Jesus was equal to the task. He encapsulated the mythopoeic in his actions. He was the incarnation of the ideal. The action of going to the cross, of being crucified, was symbolic. God himself showed, had to show, that he was one with the suffering of humanity. The creator of the universe had no answer for suffering but to become suffering himself. He had created the universe. It was his choice to create a universe where free will and feeling and suffering would be possible. All kinds of necessities were entailed with the creation of such a universe.

The wisdom expressed in words is acted out in reality. There can be a whole world of meaning behind a deed. It expresses outwardly what the person is inwardly: the soul expresses itself in the world. And by the outward expression of the great soul's deeds the world itself is changed forever.

Bread is a symbol of spiritual food and wine of spiritual drink. By his symbolic actions Jesus became the actual bread and wine of the spirit. The true mystery of Jesus Christ is that he is the food of the soul because he has a true link to the eternal Father, the origin and sustainer of the universe. In him the analogous was enfleshed, 'the Word became flesh.'

The revelation of the numinous

As we saw, Otto coined the word 'numinous' to speak of the peculiar awe and dread and uncanny feeling which one can have in the presence of the 'wholly other.' The Bible is full of this feeling, although, of course, it is not called numinous. Instead, words such as 'awe', 'awesome', 'glory', 'glorious', 'holiness', 'holy', 'judgment', 'judge' are used. But, of course, we must not forget that along with the *mysterium tremendum* and the 'astonishment that strikes us dumb, amazement absolute' of Otto, there is the contrast of 'love' and 'joy.' 'God comes in awesome majesty' says Elihu to Job[13] but again and again in the Bible the kingdom of God is a kingdom of joy. 'You will fill me with joy in your presence, with eternal pleasures at your right hand,' says David.[14]

The Jews had a genius for being aware of the numinous. It was not merely an internal feeling, important as these feelings were. It was something that came to them from outside themselves. They recognised what was happening as God revealing himself to them. He was their God – the God who had created the heavens and the earth – they were his covenant people. This God is not something wholly transcendent, unknowable. He is eminently immanent. He is a personal God who speaks directly to people. The God who took them from Egypt to Canaan, the land of promise, by miraculous and momentous signs and deeds. He is the God who, despite being transcendent, makes himself understood to the person who trusts in him.

Unlike the gods of the neighbouring tribes, the numinous God was the unseen God. When he spoke from Mount Sinai, he warned the people through Moses not to come too near the mountain, or that they would be consumed. The people were terrified; 'they trembled with fear.' 'The people remained at a distance, while Moses approached the thick darkness where God was.'[15] He is so holy that people were not allowed near to where he was revealing himself. The same happened with Joshua, the leader who led the Israelites to Canaan. The people weren't allowed to come within a thousand yards of the Ark of the Covenant. God was with the ark and would stop the waters of the Jordan so that the people could pass to the other side.

God spoke directly to Joshua, the military leader of the Israelites, as he had spoken to Moses. In effect, he told him and his troops to destroy the cities of Canaan. They erased Jericho. 'They devoted the city to the Lord and destroyed with the sword every living thing in it – men and women, young and old, cattle sheep and donkeys.'[16] The same happened to the cities of Makkedah, Libnah, Lachish, Eglon, Debir and Hebron. Joshua subdued the whole region. 'He left no survivors. He totally destroyed all who breathed, just as the Lord, the God of Israel had commanded.'[17]

From a 21st century perspective this seems all but incredible. How could a loving God recommend the merciless destruction of young children? Above all, how can this God be reconciled with the God of love revealed in Jesus Christ? It can surely only be reconciled if we believe that God was revealing himself progressively. Man is a fallen creature. He is a child of his time. It is possible, even probable, that the Israelites only dimly perceived what God intended. These were the actions of fallen man.

Although God was speaking to them, they were still apparently victims of the brutal tribal morality of the late Bronze Age. Nevertheless, despite all the dreadful brutality, God revealed himself to them as a numinous presence doing miraculous deeds. Perhaps it was their interpretation of this numinous presence that was wrong. We also have to remember that when the Israelites 'did evil in the eyes of the Lord', they were equally punished. They were constantly backsliding and worshiping idols and forgetting the true God and God was consequently meting out judgment to them. They were not above the law.

Later, with the prophets, God is portrayed as a God of mercy. The Lord tells Jeremiah to proclaim the message, 'Return, faithless Israel ... for I am merciful.'[18] Daniel declares, 'The Lord our God is merciful and forgiving, even though we have rebelled against him ....'[19] He is a God who keeps 'his covenant of love.'[20] Gradually, through a people, the Jews, through their history, God is revealing himself as a loving, merciful God. He uses specific people, the prophets, who are close to him and have an awareness of his presence, to reveal himself as he truly is. This in turn has meaning for human behaviour. Man should strive to be perfect as he is perfect. God's revelation of himself was to be revealed in a sinless man, Jesus Christ.

Jesus – the numinous in human form

In complete contrast to the morality of Joshua's time is the morality of Jesus. The military leader had no scruples about extinguishing all life in a captured city and dealing with the enemy mercilessly. Jesus, on the other hand, said: 'Love your enemies and pray for those who persecute you, that you may be the sons of your Father in heaven.'[21] The sermon on the mount, from which the quote comes, is such a radically new way of approaching the human / divine that it is little wonder that many Jews were nonplussed. Yet some of them were chosen by Jesus himself to be taught and to understand: those he called the disciples.

Jesus is the Greek form of Joshua, the name given to Mary's firstborn son. It means 'The Lord saves.' It was a common name among the Jews. Nothing could be more salutary than the contrast between the first Joshua and the second. Joshua had numinous events in his life to herald and confirm his leadership of Israel. With Jesus, he himself is the numinous in human form. God decides to reveal himself in a man. Jesus had a peculiarly close relationship to the transcendent, so close that the transcendent appeared to shine in and through him. And yet he was a man through and through. He could suffer and feel pain and tiredness.

Numinous, transcendent, yes. But the God revealed is so, so different to Joshua's God. Not at all the God the early Jewish nation looked up to. Not a God of strength, overpowering his enemies, but a God of weakness, a God of the negative. He emptied himself, became nothing. He became one with suffering humanity, the suffering God. This was so counter-intuitive. No wonder the traditionally-minded Jews couldn't believe he was God. He who countermanded all previous conceptions of God.

The numinous is often accompanied by the miraculous, and so it was with Jesus. Thirty-three miracles by him are recorded in the Gospels, twenty-three of which are healings. Blind people receive their sight and lepers are healed. The miracles are meant to be a sign that he is from God: '... even if you do not believe me, believe the miracles, that you may understand that the Father is in me, and I in the Father.'[22] The miracles are partly what give him the quality of the numinous. It caused amazement: 'What kind of man is this?'[23]

But, of course, the words he speaks contribute to the feeling of amazement. The parables of the kingdom have profound meaning and people struggle to understand them. It will only be after the resurrection that even the disciples will begin to get a glimpse and then fully understand who has been with them. Then it begins to all fall into place. They have been in the centre of the historic struggle between the powers of light and darkness. God has revealed himself in the form of man, in the form of weakness, shoulder to shoulder with man in his weakness and pain. The second Adam. And only afterwards does he reveal himself in glorious power as the resurrected Lord. Indeed, the Lord of the cosmos.

The cosmic Christ

That is another step, and it is the apostle John who makes the cosmic significance most clear. Jesus 'was with God in the beginning.'[24] 'Through him all things were made; without him nothing was made that has been made.'[25] Here already in the 1st century, there is a fully developed theology. Jesus Christ is fully man: he is also somehow fully God. God in Christ, the Logos, was the creator who brought order to the cosmos. The absolutely sacred, God himself, reveals itself in the form of a man. The Sacred, the truly numinous, reveals itself in the world of the profane. And the answer of the profane is to murder the Sacred, to attempt to annihilate it. But, of course, the Sacred cannot be annihilated, because it is the source of all that is. Rather it is resurrected in its true numinous power.

This is a stupendous vision. Even more stupendous when viewed from the perspective of modern scientific discoveries. With his limited scientific knowledge, the psalmist could consider the glory of the heavens 'the work of your fingers.' How much more so can we marvel at the wonders displayed by modern astronomy. The vast number of galaxies, the billions of stars. Everything marvellously precise. All stemming from an instant some 14 billion years ago.

And on our own planet earth, at the molecular and atomic levels we see the same precision. And that precision and differentiation as revealed by the periodic table of the elements is reflected in everything we perceive by our senses. Elements which had their origin in the precise nuclear processes of ancient stars. Senses which have become conscious of their own origin.

Now, wherever in the world we are, we can sit and consider the works of the Lord. What the world of science has revealed to us is even more miraculous than the ancient psalmist realised. And yet many people tend to be a lot more blasé about the world around them than the ancients were, because they think of it in terms of a naturalistic process.

As I sat on my own in a restaurant recently waiting for Margaret to get out of hospital, I thought about the things around me. I don't mean the chairs, tables, candles and all the other objects and items. All these man-made objects and artefacts will one day go out of existence. What I mean are the apparent substances of which the objects are made. I say 'apparent' because the very idea of 'substance' is a construction of the mind, a useful metaphor for what we see in front of us. In reality, if we were small enough to see the 'interior' of an atom, we would see that it was empty space, or an energy field with non-local effects. It is not 'substance' but meaning, interacting with all the other limitless atoms of meaning.

So this meaning-substance, which is wood, of which the table is made, was once a tree, a part of organic life. It got its energy from the sun by means of photosynthesis and chemical nutrients from the soil via its roots. The sun itself is part of stellar evolution which can be traced back to the origins of the cosmos itself. But the point is that everything was there *potentially* from the very beginning. The steel in the candle-stand came once upon a time from nuclear reactions in the interior of a star. The water in the glass – that miracle liquid – the deceptively simple one, is also eternal in its roots. In all the objects around me I see not the object but the eternal meaning-substance. The once-created that issued from the eternal and that now leaps out at me in its primal significance.

When seen and appreciated from their aspect of origin, their eternal origin, all meaning-substances glow with a numinous intensity. They are in the here and now, a constant presence for every human consciousness, but they also reverberate and resonate with the ever-present story of their eternal origin. To sit and contemplate the meaning-substances of which things are made is what I mean by saying to 'consider the works of the Lord.' And the Lord is both God and the Logos, Christ the Lord. As it says in John, he was there 'from the beginning.'

I contrast this appreciation of 'matter' with that which I had when I was a young lad. When my hand brushed against wood, it was only wood, a mere natural material. So it was with all substances. Now, as I have tried to show, I see them in a different light – and it all begins to make sense. And rather than the world and universe being 'dead' matter, it is the numinous garment of the living God. Not God himself, but God's creation. A creation of glorious intensity.

Prophecies

We have seen how Jung considered synchronicities, or meaningful coincidences, to be an indication of a 'cross-connection of events' that 'cannot be explained causally.' We are used to thinking of meaning 'as a psychic process or content that it never enters our heads to suppose that it could also exist outside the psyche.'[26] He was talking about how dreams, for example, can coincide with something happening in the 'real' world. It was as if the transcendental was giving a person a message by linking something 'mental' with something 'physical.' When such events happen to us personally, we are amazed, because such occurrences are outwith the power of the psyche to effect. They appear to be outwith 'natural' laws. And yet they appear to have meaning for the individual concerned.

Now prophecies appear to be a special form of synchronicity. The big difference is that the mental event, that is, the dream from the Lord or the Lord speaking to the prophet, happens a long time before the physical event. And the physical event happens to someone else. With synchronicity the different types of events tend to happen in the experience of the one person. But to me it seems to be much more amazing that a prediction of a future event could be made. Who knows what the future holds? Unless it is the infinite-divine.

Yet this is precisely what we get with the Messianic prophecies. And it is not just one prophecy but a conglomeration of prophecies that are fulfilled in the life and death of Jesus. These prophecies were made hundreds of years before Jesus appeared on earth. Perhaps it was Isaiah who made the most striking prophecies and he began his ministry in 740 B.C., the year that King Uzziah died. But it is not just Isaiah; the expectation of a Messiah and of a Messianic age is implicit or explicit in much of the scriptures and consciousness of the Jews.

They are a special people, and considered themselves a chosen people, chosen by God to reveal himself to the world, both to the Jews themselves and to the Gentiles. In retrospect, it is easy to see how this has happened in the person of Jesus Christ. But 3000 years ago it was not at all clear what would happen 1000 years hence. Yet the clues are there, in the Torah and in the prophets.

The serpent in Genesis 3.15 is symbolic of the battle between good and evil in the hearts of men and women. God says to the serpent: 'And I will put enmity between you and the woman, and between your offspring and hers; he will crush your head, and you will strike his heel.' This is often seen as a prediction of Christ's overthrow of Satan and his kingdom of evil. God chooses Abram and says to him that 'all peoples on earth will be blessed through you.'[27] Hundreds of years later, in the time of the exodus, the Passover lamb is seen (in the 1st century AD) as predictive and symbolic of the death of Jesus, 'The Lamb of God, who takes away the sin of the world.'[28]

The nature and role of the Messiah becomes even more explicit in the book of Psalms and in the Prophets. Psalm 22 and Isaiah 53 are key texts. For Isaiah the coming saviour was not to be a great and powerful king but a person who 'was despised and rejected by men' and who 'was led like a lamb to the slaughter.' No-one who reads Isaiah 53 in the context of the Jesus story can fail to be impressed by the uncanny resemblance between the figure portrayed by the prophet and the figure of Jesus Christ as portrayed in the Gospels. The same can be said for Psalm 22 which speaks of the suffering king: 'I can count all my bones; people stare and gloat over me. They divide my garments among them and cast lots for my clothing.' Psalm 69 says 'They put gall in my food and gave me vinegar for my thirst.' The four gospels tell that while on the cross Jesus was given wine vinegar to drink.

What appear to be specific predictions are also made by other Old Testament prophets. Micah, a contemporary of Isaiah, predicts where God's ruler over Israel will be born: 'But you, Bethlehem Ephrathath, though you are small among the clans of Judah, out of you will come for me one who will be ruler over Israel, whose origins are of old, from ancient times.'[29] The coming of the Anointed One is also predicted in Daniel 9.25–27 where he says that 'the Anointed One will be cut off and will have nothing. The people of the ruler who will come will destroy the city and the sanctuary.' This latter an apparent reference to the destruction of Jerusalem by Titus in AD 70.

Examples of such prophecies could be multiplied and they are indicative of something strange: namely, that prophets knew hundreds of years in advance what was going to happen in a specific province, Palestine, and also the specific things that were going to happen to a specific individual. When these events happened, some Jews claimed them to be the fulfilment of the prophecies while others said Jesus was a false prophet and not the Anointed One. One of the reasons that the latter disbelieved was because this prophet claimed too much. He claimed God for his Father and that he could give eternal life to his followers, and so they wanted to stone him.[30] Despite all odds, believers in the prophet as the Anointed One would in the end become much more numerous.

This extraordinary story, of God taking part in human history and using the Jews to tell his story, would not be nearly as credible were it not part of the history of a people and God's extraordinary dealings with them as recorded in their scriptures, and these include the prophecies. This gives the story of Jesus as God's messenger to mankind a specificity and a depth which it wouldn't otherwise have. If synchronicities are taken as the eternal breaking through into time, how much more so are Messianic prophecies and their subsequent fulfilment?

Taking everything into account, the build-up and the accomplishment, one is persuaded that a naturalistic explanation is just not possible, but that a transcendent explanation is necessary. That Jesus was the person he claimed to be, an incarnation of the divine in human form.

• 19 •

What is truth? – (4)

The relevance of the supernatural

I couldn't have written this chapter twenty or even ten years ago. From a young age I was so influenced by naturalism and the 'scientific' point of view that I took it almost for granted that when we died that was it, *finis*, end of story. It appeared to be so obvious that when you die and your remains are placed under the ground, then the person that was *you* is no more. Your personality was part of the chemistry and genetic inheritance which was your body, of your upbringing and social milieu. How was it even sensible in any way to talk of a continuation? Common sense tells us that the end of the body is also the end of everything that accompanied the body, including the mind. At that time the idea of resurrection just seemed crazy as was the idea of the personality in some manner continuing after death.

What has made me change my mind? Let me say at the outset that it is not fear. Some might think, 'Och, he's getting older and realises he hasn't far to go. The fear of death is really concentrating his mind!' I have long faced the reality of death in that sense. Many a time in my youth I had been annoyed by sermonising from the pulpit about death. Such sermons seem to presume that people are stupid or insensitive to the facts of life – the chief fact being that we are all going to die. We all know we're going to die. What we don't know for certain is what lies beyond. A lot of people are convinced, as I used to be, that nothing lies beyond.

So what has made me change my mind? The answer is the evidence which I have given in this book. The careful reader will have noticed that, humanly speaking, it is not one thing but a concatenation of events and investigations that have led me to change my world view. The key questions for anyone with even a vague interest in the issue are: first, Can the origin of the universe and everything we see around us be explained in scientific and naturalistic terms? Second, Are there evidences and strong hints of a supernatural side to things and of a supernatural origin to the universe? For me, the answer to the first question is a definite 'No' and my answer to the second a definite 'Yes.'

The findings of modern science itself place grave doubts on the idea that the incredible world it reveals could have arisen out of so-called dead matter, even given an infinite length of time. This is particularly evident in the fields of astrophysics and molecular biology. Everything appears dovetailed to the nth degree. And that dovetailing is only possible if there are universal laws which minutely govern the matter of the universe. The big question is, 'Where did those laws come from?' Did they spring into existence on their own? I suggest that it's easier to believe that a live rabbit will come out of the hat without the aid of a magician.

But for me personally, the clincher is that *there is a side to the world that is supernatural*, that is, things that cannot be explained in terms of natural law. Partly, I have come to this conclusion because of things that have happened to me personally, and latterly to Margaret and me, and which I have recounted in this book. Similar things have happened to numerous other people. *Now, if only one of these occurrences is true, we do not live in a naturalistic universe.* For, according to scientific and naturalistic theory, everything that happens must happen according to the natural laws of the universe. If something happens which is not governed by these laws, then the world we live in has influences coming from 'outwith' the time/space universe. And these demand an explanation.

As I've just said, what happened to Margaret and me has convinced me that there is a supernatural side to things and not only a supernatural side, but a superintending supernatural side. To many, this may appear appalling, appalling because, if they came to believe it, it would mean a reappraisal of the meaning of life, and of their own life. It would not be a mere inconvenience but a major shift in thinking and lifestyle.

This shift has occurred for me. I have turned from being an agnostic to being a Christian. The supernatural events that have occurred in my life have meant that I have gone back to the Bible. And there I find a stupendous claim – the claim that God has revealed himself through the human being Jesus Christ. Part of the revelation was a supernatural event which we call the resurrection. The resurrection, more than any other event recorded in the Bible, puts us on the spot. We either have to believe it or not believe it.

It really gets to the heart of the matter as no other event does. In Corinthians, 15.14 the Apostle Paul says, '... if Christ has not been raised, our preaching is useless and so is your faith.' What Paul is in effect saying is that without the resurrection the Christian message is a naturalistic message, however highly moral or inspiring. We have to take the resurrection in conjunction with what Jesus was claiming about himself. To the contemporary learned Jews – including Saul of Tarsus who was to become the Apostle Paul – his claims that he came from the Father were outrageous. He was making himself equal with God.

His claims *were* outrageous. But the resurrection was even more outrageous. And so it still proves to be for many people. And yet it is either true or it is not true, just as we can say, 'It is either true or not true that there are supernatural events occurring even in today's world.' But, equally, we can say, 'There is either a God or there isn't a God.' Such a statement is linked to the supernatural question. And if there is a God, the resurrection of a dead body should be easy for him. Certainly it would appear to be easy in comparison to the creation of the universe! So by saying, 'I don't believe in the resurrection' we are begging the question of whether there is a God or not.

This whole either/or question came home to me recently as I stood with a poet friend in the churchyard of Dornoch cathedral, originally built in the 13th century, almost totally destroyed in 1570, but now rebuilt. As we surveyed the ancient graves, some mere stumps in the ground, some with the writing completely erased by weathering, some partially legible though covered with moss, 'From nothingness to nothingness' my friend commented softly.

I felt the weight of this comment, this nothingness which he felt. The graveyard scene could be repeated a million times throughout the world. People had been, lived happy or unhappy lives, and completely disappeared from this world of time and were now erased from human memory. All that was left was the stone and the moss.

There was one 19th century stone with the name John Ross, shoemaker, died aged 77. His wife had died at the age of 39. His three children had died within a few years of each other. The bare facts spoke volumes. I imagined him as a widower carrying on working at his last. Was he full of regrets and sorrow to the end? We will never know.

But the gravestones, all with their implicit sorrow, were all question marks. They all begged the question, either it is case of 'nothingness to nothingness', as my friend said, or there is something more. Either this world is naturalistic and self-contained and death is the absolute end or it is underpinned by a transcendent infinite. If the latter, then death is not the end, although standing in a graveyard it might appear so. I have given the reasons why the apparent 'nothingness' is not a nothingness at all but is full of meaning because it is from, in and through an infinite transcendent spirit/mind.

We have seen that there is a lot of evidence from the created world for the existence of a supernatural being. The prophecies made about the coming of a messiah, the dealings of God with the Jews, the life and sayings of Jesus and the resurrection itself are all further proof of a superintendent and immanent deity.

Many people will of course doubt that such an event as the resurrection ever took place. But how many of these people will have looked in detail at the evidence for the resurrection. Probably less than 1%. They will be, as I was at one time, governed by the presumption of naturalism. Gary R. Habermas, a distinguished scholar and recognised authority on the resurrection, has studied the case for the historicity of the resurrection over a period of thirty years. He has come to the firm conclusion that the bodily resurrection of Jesus was a reality for the disciples.[1]

Using a 'minimal facts' approach and the latest scholarship techniques he demonstrates clearly the great likelihood that the bodily resurrection of Jesus took place. The 'minimal facts' approach concentrates on 'data which are strongly evidenced' and which 'are granted by virtually all scholars on the subject, even the sceptical ones.'[2] These four facts, which are accepted by nearly every scholar of the subject, are, 1. That Jesus died by crucifixion 2. His disciples really believed that he appeared to them 3. Paul, the despiser of Christians and persecutor of the church was suddenly changed and 4. The sceptic James, brother of Jesus, and who up to then had rejected his brother's claims to divinity, was suddenly changed. The fifth fact is also important, that of the empty tomb. 'Roughly 75 per cent of scholars on the subject accept the empty tomb as a historical fact.'[3]

On the basis of these five facts alone Habermas builds up a strong case that the resurrection took place as recorded in the Gospels. This is not the place to detail his use of sources and subtle arguments but it should be made clear that Habermas makes his case not just from the Biblical text but from other ancient texts, whether Jewish or Roman. In an impressive earlier volume, *The Historical Jesus, Ancient Evidence for the life of Christ*, he employs the same stringent historical research tools to establish the historicity of Jesus, using non-Christian sources in addition to the Scriptures themselves.

So we come back to the question posed by Pilate to Jesus, 'What is truth?' and it turns out to be something totally unexpected. Not the truth of philosophy or science, of the arts or even of theology but the truth encapsulated in a person. When Jesus said, 'I am the way, the truth and the life. No-one comes to the Father except through me',[4] he was saying something both simple and profound. The truth as it is in Jesus is the truth of a relationship, that between Christ – the Son, the Logos, the Word – and God the eternal Origin. We can participate in this eternal Origin only through believing in the incarnation, that is, that God was incarnated in the flesh of human form.

The Christ-truth is the truth about how we relate to God and to other human beings and even to the natural world. Love is declared to be the fulfilment of the law or what the Jews called righteousness. Christ fulfilled the law to the letter and so had perfect righteousness. He fully transcended the ego and the selfish self and gave himself wholly for others. By sacrificing himself he demonstrated that God, the Origin, is love. God becomes most transparently immanent in the suffering of Christ. He became one with suffering humanity. He was the new spiritual root for those who would be born of the spirit, those who would believe that all is not nothingness. Rather the infinite in Christ is a plenitude of life.

As we have seen, everything, or any individual thing we choose to consider, goes back to God, the Origin. The truths as seen through any of the modes which Dooyeweerd identifies – modes such as linguistic, analytical-logical, historical and so on – are only partial truths. Any one of these truths is a distortion of the whole truth. Only through the mode of faith can we appreciate the truth as it is given in Jesus Christ. Just as God gave and revealed himself in history as a free gift in Christ, so the faith in him is also a free gift. What the Bible calls the 'heart' is the link between God and the human being, between the eternal and man. But only by believing in Christ and accepting the Holy Spirit can the process of heart-cleansing begin and the link – broken in the Fall, in the breaking away from the Origin – between God and the human root be re-established.

This process can be experienced by anyone who accepts Jesus as the Son of God and acknowledges him. In the New Testament this process of acknowledgement is known as 'believing and being baptised.' Paul, the apostle to the Gentiles, say in Romans 8:16, 'The Spirit himself testifies with our spirit that we are God's children.'

· 20 ·

Conclusions

(1) Myles

For me the search for the truth has been a long and tortuous road. It has been a journey from a belief in the naturalism of things to a conviction that there is a transcendent side to the world which reveals itself in various ways; a conviction that there is a reality outside of time and space. I have tried to show what has led me to this conviction. The doubts I had concerning naturalism first occurred to me because of synchronistic events which happened to me personally and from my reading of Jung. Then there were the intuitions I had that the creation around me, and even the most mundane of materials, was in essence miraculous. This was reinforced in a major way by the discoveries of science in the last 50 years.

Then there were the supernatural – for want of a better word – events that happened to me personally before I met Margaret. But what has really clinched the matter for me, and made me believe in a personal God who deals personally (that is, relates) with people, are the events that have happened since Margaret phoned me in the year 2000. Some might brush off the meaningful coincidences and supernatural events that I've recounted with a shrug of the shoulders. That, of course, is their free choice and right.

Their effect on me has been profound. For me they were not just any old supernatural event (if there could be such a category). They were in a context. And they were intimately connected with what was happening in my life. Margaret, who had the dream, was a Christian when she got in touch with me. And what happened happened in a Christian context, for example, the fall of the stick led to the Bunyan incident and the finding of *Pilgrim's Progress* in the loft. All that happened has led me to believe that everything is interconnected and that everything has meaning. It is a world of hope rather than despair.

The whole sequence of events as described in this book has led me to believe, first, that there is superintending deity who has intimate knowledge of everything about us, second, that the deity cares about us, third, that he gives us freedom to choose how we relate to him and others, fourth, that it is only when we believe in him and trust him that he will reveal himself to us, fifth, that this life is not the end of the story, sixth, that he revealed himself through Jesus Christ, seventh, that the resurrection is real and that that is why this life is not the end of the story.

The question of trust is absolutely central to the matter. I don't merely mean trust between people, although that is important. It is a trust that there is a transcendent Being that is outwith time and space and which is yet immanent and can enter and influence the space-time continuum; who is also the ground of our being and who has given us being. Not only that, but that humans can have a relation with this Being. The whole question of this kind of trust has to be seen against the backdrop of European philosophy. Kant held that space and time are intuitional modes by which humans order what they perceive around them. For him natural laws were part and parcel of how our minds organise reality. Reason could not prove the existence of God or the soul or even human freedom. Man becomes the centre of his world. No wonder it ended in the existentialism of despair. All we can talk about are appearances, not the noumena, or how things really are in themselves.

Reason then is not the answer. But what if there is a Being outside of space and time – indeed the creator of their possibility – and who can communicate with creatures living in space-time. In this book I have given reasons why I think we can fully trust that there is such a Being. The beauty and power which shines so translucently through nature, meaningful coincidences, the sense of the numinous and the sometimes overpowering sense of the sacred, the feeling for the moral and good, supernatural events and the findings of science all point to a Being beyond time. These all cry out for us to trust in ultimate meaning.

But even more remarkable than any of these, the transcendent, God, what is beyond phenomena, has revealed himself to mankind in the life, death and resurrection of Jesus Christ. He chose one people, the Jews, and one man, long fore-shadowed, to show himself and his true nature to humankind. God says that by trusting absolutely in Jesus that we also can trust absolutely in him. By trusting in Jesus he reveals himself to us and comes to live in our hearts. By revealing himself in Jesus he makes a statement: that he is objectively personal and can relate to the human, that he is not an impersonal it, but is a pan- and trans-personal being.

The struggles I recounted in Chapters 15 and 16 are over. We now trust each other absolutely. The only reason we have told of our difficulties is that they might bring others to faith in the existence of God and a transcendent reality. It was not an easy decision to tell some of the things which happened to us. For me, personally, I tell it because it sheds light on a question which is relevant to a lot of people, namely, the nature of reality itself.

I continue to be overwhelmed by the paradox that it was because of lack of trust in each other that God led us to trust in him. The fact that I have finally put my trust in Christ, I am sure has something to do with it. I have the feeling that things were meant to be. What I mean by that is that God out of a profound mercy has bothered to turn a pathetic specimen like me to himself and has given me a faith in him. This continually amazes me! He could have left me to stew in my own juice of rationalism and naturalism. To the contrary my rationalism has been overturned and my belief in naturalism found wanting. The trust I have is directly from him: it has nothing whatsoever to do with me. In a thousand lifetimes I could not have engineered it.

By nothing less than what is to me a miracle, he gave me in my life just what was required to bring me to faith. I was such a thrawn unbelieving person that only what I have recounted could have done that. Whatever happens next, I am convinced that nothing can separate us from the love of God outside time and space and which was revealed in time in Jesus Christ.

(2) Margaret

As I look back on all that has happened, for me it is all so amazing. On many occasions, the journey I have been on has not been an easy one, but I have learned to rely on God in all things. We are all sinners in thought, word and deed.

The process of becoming better, or to use the old theological term, sanctification, is an ongoing process and it is very often through tough experiences that we learn. For me it was a process of pruning but I look back now and realise that there were a number of things I had to deal with, namely, my stubbornness, and lack of patience, Also, I would hand things over for God to deal with but then take them back and try and deal with them in my own way. A Christian will not get away with a foot on either side of the fence. It doesn't work.

I believe that I had to go through what happened in order to grow into a deeper relationship with God and to strengthen my faith. I had to learn to rely on God at all times in everything instead of when it suited me. I marvel at how close he is to us and his knowledge of what refining we all need to go through to make us into what he wants us to be.

PART 2

Tìr a' Gheallaidh

Sreath-dhàn

Maoilios Caimbeul

Phòs Daibhaidh agus Ioanna nuair a bha iad nam meadhan aois. Choinnich iad an toiseach nuair a bha ise 17 agus esan 19, ach dhealaich an slighean agus cha do choinnich iad a-rithist airson 36 bliadhna. 'S ann air sàillibh aisling a bh' aig Ioanna a choinnich iad a-rithist agus a phòs iad. Bha Ioanna a' creidsinn gur ann bho Dhia a bha an aisling. Bliadhnaichean às dèidh dhaibh pòsadh, bha iad a' bruidhinn air leabhar a sgrìobhadh mu na thachair dhaibh. Bha Daibhidh teagmheach mu chùisean creideimh agus gum urrainn nithean os-nàdarra tachairt. Gus aon latha agus iad air a bhith sia bliadhna pòsta ...

1

Bha e mar latha sam bith eile,
an latha a thuit am maide;
bha iad nan suidhe aig am biadh
sa chidsin agus thuirt e rithe –
'S dòcha gum bu chòir dhuinn an leabhar a sgrìobhadh.
'S dòcha, thuirt i, 's dòcha gum bu chòir.
Agus thuit am maide.

Cha bu chòir dha tuiteam, cha robh ann ach maide,
maide gun bheatha, gun deò, gun treòir, gun mhothachadh.
'S e maide fada a bh' ann airson doras an lobht fhosgladh
agus e na chrochadh air tarraig anns a' lobaidh,
airson bhliadhnaichean,

agus thuit e le gleadhraich air a' làr,
thuit e leis fhèin 's gun duine faisg air.
Thuit e nuair a thuirt Daibhidh ri a mhnaoi,
'S dòcha gum bu chòir dhuinn an leabhar a sgrìobhadh,
an leabhar mu am beatha a bha iad am beachd a sgrìobhadh,
a dh'innseadh mar a dhèilig Dia riutha,
mar a thachair iad às dèidh nam bliadhaichean mòra
air sgàth aisling a bh' aige Ioanna.

O, Ioanna, carson a bha an aisling ud agad,
carson a bhuair i thu le pian agus deòir
airson duine nach fhac' thu
airson sia bliadhna deug ar fhichead?
Carson a thuirt an searmonaiche riut?
'S ann bho Dhia a tha i. Bha an aon seòrsa
aisling agamsa, mus do choinnich mi ri mo bhean.

Bha iad nan suidhe aig a' bhòrd nuair a thuit am maide;
chuir e iongnadh mòra orra nuair a thuit e
's gun duine faisg air.
(Ann an siud air an tarraig airson sia bliadhna deug,
gun tuiteam.)

Cha robh Daibhidh toilichte.
Dhorchnaich a chridhe le smaointean dìomhair.
An e manadh a th' ann ag iarraidh orm
an lobht fhalmhachadh?
Treallaich nam bliadhnaichean a chartadh.
An e seo a' chrìoch?
Cha bu chòir dha tachairt, maide a' tuiteam leis fhèin,
gun duine faisg air, gun ghaoth na ghaoth.

An latha ud, thàinig atharrachadh nan saoghal.
Bha dath eile air an iarmailt,
agus dath eile air an leabhar.

Seachdain às dèidh sin
a' dol gu meadhan-oidhche
agus iad a' tuiteam nan cadal
chuala iad gleadhraich san lobaidh.
Bha am maide air tuiteam a-rithist.

A Dhè nan gràs, glèidh sinn.

Làrna-mhàireach, thòisich e
a' falmhachadh an lobht.

Agus shuidh e aig an deasg a' sgrìobhadh.

2

A' cuimhneachadh nan seann làithean ...

A bheil cuimhn' agad, nuair a choinnich sinn
an Inbhir Nis air an earrach ud?
Thug thu ugh seoclaid Càisge dhomh.
Tha cuimhn' a'm, thusa seachd-deug,
nad chòta corduroy uaine,
fo na craobhan anns Na Islands
agus chuir e iongnadh ort gun tug mi ugh dhut.
Chuir e iongnadh orm fhìn gun tug mi ugh dhut,
ugh brèagha airgeadach dathte.
Ach cha tàinig nì beò às an ugh sin,
dh'fhàg thu mi airson fear eile,
chaidh thu air ais gu do chiad ghaol
agus phòs sibh agus bha clann agaibh
agus chaidh mise air turas a' mhic stròdhail.

3

Rona sin, bha e òg ann an seòmraichean gràidh.
Rona sin, bha i òg ann an seòmraichean bàidh.
Pàrantan diadhaidh gam biadhadh le slàint',

ach dhaibhsan nan cuibhrichean gan cumail bho shaorsa,
leth-bheò ann an eileanan na daorsa,
leig às mi, leig air falbh mi, b' e an glaodh.

4

Cò tha seo?

An gille beag Sgitheanach,
domhainn ann a' leabhraichean,
inntinn air sgèith le 'nam' is 'ach';

saoghal cruinn Gàidhealach,
ach lionnrachadh na mheadhan,
an sgoil na neasgaid na creich'.

Ach cò tha seo a' tabhann tùr,
aig an daras le leabhraichean dearga,
leabhar mòr-eòlais bho Newnes?

An gille beag le 'Bìoball' ùr,
ga shùghadh mar an lite am bainne,
Darwin's 's Freud an ceannach daor.

An leabhar dubh 's an leabhar dearg,
fuil ann an ùir nan linntinn,
's an crann a' dol na craoibh feirge.

5

Dhàsan

Tìr na fadachd às
am measg nam mucan
air a bhiadhadh le sprùilleach
is plaosgan ana-miann.

Bliadhnaichean dol seachad.

Mòr-fhàsach gun uisge
rionnagan-earbaill
smaointean gun àireamh
a' tuiteam dhan dorchadas.

Na bliadhnaichean dol seachad.

A' tuiteam an adhar
doilleir an eu-dòchais
neonitheachd air bruaich
na h-oillt is an uamhainn.

Cò a chruthaich na slèibhtean?

Fear mionaideach na reachd –
Esan fada bho a bheachd,
ach ann an ùir dhìomhair
bha sìol gun fhios dha a' fàs.

'S na bliadhnaichean dol seachad.

6

Bha cuimhn' agam ort
ged nach robh guth agam ort –
ann an cùil tharcaisich
dhe m' inntinn bha thu ann
am measg na feadhna eile.

7

Dhìse

Taigh is teaghlach
sràidean coimheach
is gaol daonnda
is corra dhaorach.

Iòsaph fada bho a dhaoine.

Luchd-tadhail às an eilean
bràithrean, peathraichean,
biadh ga ullachadh
is Dia air a' sgeilp

Iòsaph a' caoidh a dhaorsa.

8

Cha robh cuimhn' agam ort
ach mar thu fhèin
ann an cùil na neo-aire;
bha mo bheatha làn
le saothair an t-saoghail.

9

Esan

Bruadraidh e bàrdachd, glaiste ann a' smaointean,
a' dìreadh na beinne 's gun e lorg nì
ach truileis reusain nach sàsaicheadh cridhe;

na beanntan geal' ud air a' bheulaibh
's na lochan criostal air na mullaich, ma b' fhìor,
ach gan ruighinn, tiormachd is tart.

Inns dhomh gu bheil thu ann, chanadh e,
os cionn na gile 's nan eun 's a' mhiann,
's dheigheadh e dhachaigh le droch bhlas na bheul.

Dheigheadh e a shealg na h-èilde gil
's bhiodh i dol glan às a shealladh,
thar an droma mar nach robh i idir ann.

Aon latha sheas e air beulaibh na falamhachd
agus thuirt e gu dùbhlanach, dearbh dhomh
gu bheil thu ann, siuthad dearbh dhomh;

cha robh ann ach beanntan a' bhrosnachaidh,
ach sheall e sìos agus fa chomhair air a' bhòrd
air soitheach-luaithre bha na facail sgrìobhte

'An Dùbhlan.'

**Às dèidh bliadhnaichean sa bhaile mhòr, thill Ioanna gu
eilean a breith agus a h-àraich ...**

10

Fhad 's a bhruadair e bàrdachd, bhruadair i tilleadh
às a' bhaile dhùmhail gu a h-eilean, gu tobar
a dòchais, Iòsaph a' tighean dhachaigh mu dheireadh
bho thìr na fadachd às, luchdaichte le saidhbhreas.

A h-athair 's na bràithrean a' feitheamh thall.
Dhìrich ise beanntan cuideachd agus monaidhean
nam boglaichean, uamhan is slocan air an t-slighe,
gun seasamh coise sa chrèadh 's a' chlàbar.

Gun i 'g iarraidh turas ri eaglais – ìomhaighean
dubha, cleòcaichean cruaidh an ùghdarrais –
'na geàrr d' fhalt, na seall gràdh aig doras eaglais' –
riaghailtean uachdrach a' seachnadh an dìomhair.

Ann an adhar a bha i an dòchas a bhiodh gorm,
dh'èirich sgòthan brùideil dubha air fàire,
gaoth is doineann ga caitheamh gu làidir
mar bhàta pàipeir air a sracadh o chèile.

Ghlèidh i a h-athair gu a h-uchd is e aig uchd bàis,
a h-Iàcob dha robh a gràdh cho mòr,

e air falbh leis an t-sruth ann an onfhadh na mara,
ise air a toinneadh ann an sumainnean dòrainn.

Ann an teanntachd anam, air chrith le uamhann,
na h-èiginn dh'fhosgail i an leabhar agus leugh i:
Bi sàmhach 's tuigibh gur mi Dia. 'S am priobadh,
thàinig fois gu a corp agus sìth gu a h-anam.

Dh'fhalbh uallaichean nam bliadhnaichean 's thuirt i:
Tha an t-eòlas seo robh iongantach
Is ormsa tha e cruaidh; cha ruig mi air,
Oir tha e àrd r' a thuigsinn is r' a luaidh.

'S mu dheireadh nuair a chaidh i dhan eaglais –
a dh'aindeoin uireasbhaidh a' chomainn sin –
bha e mar gu robh e a' leughadh a smuain,
an searmon a' mion-fhrithealadh a feum.

**Bha Daibhidh air chall airson bhliadhnaichean am measg
fheallsanachdan agus chreideamhan, a' sireadh gun a bhith
a' lorg ...**

11

Esan agus an Guth

Tha mi coiseachd gu dòlasach
air sligean briste a' chridhe,
mo bhuinn air an gearradh
agus fuil a' tighinn asta.

Thuirt an guth, ma tha mu thogair,
do choire mhòr fhèin a th' ann,
nach tuirt d' athair mus do dh'fhàg thu,
'Cuir d' earbs' an Dia, 's leanaidh maith riut.'

Ach chaidh thu slighe nam beann 's chladaich,
an t-slighe sheachranach chrìon. Shaltair
do chasan na dìtheanan naomha,
dh'òl thu à puill ghrod shaillte do mhiann.

Bhrist reusan mo chreideamh,
bha a h-uile nì nàdarrach;
muir a' briseadh air cladach gun truas,
na h-ionracain gan spadadh gun deòir.

Na cuir d' earbs' anns a' chladach
no ann an uachdar na mara;
bidh am foghlam fada ach ruigidh tu
na doimhneachdan ann an latha na tròcair.

Nuair a bhios a' ghealach slàn
os cionn a' chuain, fo shùil na sìorraidheachd,
chì thu an dealbh shlàn,
agus gach nì crìochnaichte.

12

Na h-Aodainn

E coiseachd a's a' choille,
aodainn os a chionn a' deàrrsadh
le solas àrsaidh soilleir;

aodainn na gealaich nach robh e tuigsinn
ga shireadh 's ga thathaich
bhon rìoghachd chèin do-ruigsinn;

am ministear air Sràid an Dòchais –
's e an Glaschu còmhla ri athair –
aodann làn gràis agus sòlais,

plathadh à tìr nach tuig e,
agus an-còmhnaidh aodann a mhàthar
na ceist shìorraidh air nach ruig e;

agus a' mhaighdean òg le fiamh
tar-dhìreachdail na gnùis,
mar gum biodh mar dhìthean bho riamh;

agus a' bhean dlùth dhan bhàs
le sìth do-thuigsinneach na sùilean,
is fios ro mhath aic' air a càs;

agus aogas athar sa chiste
mar gum biodh e dìreach air coinneachadh
ris a' chruthaidhear gun fhiosta.

Aodainn ga thathaich, aodainn na gealaich,
plathaidhean gràis ga bhualadh,
ga bhuaireadh, 's a' dol à sealladh.

13

Seach gun urrainn dhan t-sìorraidheachd briseadh air tìm,
seach gu bheil i sin so-shuainte sa chridhe,
seach gu bheil an t-aodann ann an tìm agus às,
thoir sùil air a gnùis nuair a bhruidhneas tu rithe.

Thoir sùil air an aodann nuair a bhruidhneas tu ris,
cuir na ceistean ort fhèin, na feith ris a-màireach:
San eadar-aodann tha seo, cò tha bruidhinn rium?
Cò leis an solas a tha soillseachadh gàire?

Cò às a dh'èirich an ròs tha beannachadh àile?
Tha am mise 's an tusa mar cheistean dha chèile.
Tha spiorad neo-thalmhaidh a' cluich na do shùilean,
chan e gràdh ach doimhneachd na cruinne tha mi leughadh.

**Às dèidh bhliadhnaicheann ann an eilean a h-àraich,
dh'fhàg Ioanna airson a dhol a dh'obair Shasainn ...**

14

Tha mi sgìth dhe seo,
tha mi tinn le seo,
air mo dhearg thachdadh –
's chunnaic i an cladach tro na deòir.

Thàinig i subhach ann
is dh'fhalbh i dubhach às:
pian an dealachaidh
is tonnan a' bhruaillein.

Eilean a cuid deòir,
eilean a tròcair
's e falbh bhuaipe air fàire
mar a sheòl am bàta,

mar a sheòl a h-anam
gu dùthaich eile
's chitheadh i Canàan air a cùlaibh
is Èipheit a tùirse.

Ann an Cranleigh ann a' Surrey,
air falbh bho ghamhlas,
a' frithealadh seann fheadhainn,
sìth Dhè agus sàmhchair.

15

An Tilleadh

Chaidh bliadhnaichean seachad,
sìth agus àmhghar, aig an deireadh,
agus thill i a-rithist, na banntraich,

gu eilean a breith agus a h-àraich.
Thug a bràthair dhi an t-seann dhachaigh
agus thòisich i ga càradh.

A Dhè na tròcair,
cùm rium mo chiall;
tha an t-slighe doirbh
's do chlaidheamh geur;
ach tha cuideachd
faclan cofhurtachd
a' sruthadh bhod bheul.
Bidh mo chridhe
an taobh a-staigh dhìom
làn gàirdeachais
ri do sgeul.
Seinnidh m' anam
òran nuadh
mar uiseig nan speur.
Ò, seinnidh m' anam
òran nuadh
mar uiseig nan speur.

16

An Aisling

An oidhch' ud a bha an aisling agam,
chaidh mi dhan leabaidh tùrsach,
argamaid leis an luchd-càraidh
gam thilgeil far mo chùrsa.

A Dhè, carson mise, carson
a tha na tuinn gam bhualadh?
Carson a tha an saoghal seo
gam fhàgail na mo thruaghan?

Deòir is cadal luaisgeanach,
mo bheatha ga mo rùsgadh,
nuair a dhùisg an aisling mi
às nach robh mi 'g iarraidh dùsgadh.

Fear le falt liath 's a' chùl rium
gam smèideadh thighinn còmh' ris
tro gheata gu achadh uaine
far am biodh sìth agus sòlas.

Nuair a thionndaidh an t-aodann,
chunnaic mi aodann Dhaibhidh,
nas sine, ach 's e a bh' ann,
a' sìneadh a làimh dhomh.

Milis an t-sìth, rèidh an raon,
air gach taobh na craobhan uaine;
a Dhè, na leig dhomh dùsgadh,
fàg na mo chadal suain mi.

Ach dhùisg mi gu saoghal a' bhuaireis,
gu taigh a dh'fheumadh a chàradh:
bu bheag m' fhios an strì romham,
mar a dhiùltadh an aisling ud m' fhàgail.

**Bliadhnaichean a' dol seachad, Ioanna na saoghal fhèin,
Daibhidh air eilean-san. Mìle ceist ga bhuaireadh.**

17

Mic-talla san inntinn, Stalin, Pol Pot,
murt, marbhadh gach nì grod,

ainmean mar ifrinn ag èigheachd –
Biafra, Israel 's an Èipheit,

Khmer Rouge, Burundi, Indonesia
bàs is casgradh sìobhalta,

milleanan gun ainm sa ghrunnd,
am blàr gun àicheadh gun dùil.

Dè seòrsa creutair a th' annainn,
beò air feòil cho-chreutair 's mionnan?

Rwanda, Congo 's a' chòrr
mar shamh sgreataidh nar sròin;

lusan dearg' air raointean saoghail,
mùchadh gun chiall gun fhaochadh.

18

Thuirt an guth beag na chluais, *Nach fhaodadh e bhith eadar-
    dhealaichte? –*
*Athair, maith dhaibh, oir chan eil fhios aca ciod a tha iad a'
    dèanamh –*
nach fhaodadh e bhith mar an t-isean a' neadachadh àil, falaichte
na bigeinean fon sgèith, sàbhailt', gràdh gan dèanamh tèaraint'?

Cùram an àite claidheamh, sìth an àite talamh na fala,
aonadh, chan e sgaradh. Àraich an t-ionracan gu seann aois
ann an taigh a' cho-chomain. Tha sinn uile dhen aon anam,
dhen aon fhreumh, an t-aingeal is an dìabhal annainn mar aon.

Thuirt an guth beag na chluais, nach fhaodadh e bhith eadar-
    dhealaichte,
an daonnachd a' tighinn gu ìre, an ròs a' sùgradh ris an droigheann,
co-chomann nan ròs a' fàgail cùbhraidheachd air thalamh
is spiorad na sìth a' riaghladh mithean is maithean.

19

Mìorbhail an Uisge

O chunnaic   chunnaic e an t-uisge   ionganatach!
an òg-mhadainn an t-saoghail   rugadh am mìorbhail
a' sruthadh às an dìomhair   bog   trìd-shoilleir

a' còmhdach an t-saoghail   am brat dealrach
ciùin mar sgàthan   an ath mhionaid   mar bheathach beucach
doimhneachdan   làn sheòmraichean beatha   èisg gad shlìobadh

air madainn gheamhraidh   pàtranan criostail   air glainne is linne
corragan fìnealta   mìn-phàtran   obair-ghrèis dhiombuan
fìor ealain an tiotain   cinnteach   cinnteach   ris an ìre theòthachd

O uisge   is fìor do sgeul   bog mar mheileabhaid   còir
is cruaidh   brisidh tu a' chreag   a' criomadh a maitheis
an uillt 's an aibhnichean   a' giùlan eabar na beatha   gu achadh
   rèidh

is fìor do sgeul   an stuth giùlanach   làn brìgh
cagarsaich ri creig   is ceòl do shlighe dhan an tartmhor   mòr
do chaidreachas fhonn ris na dìthreibh   binneas gun mheang

chunnaic   chunnaic e an t-uisge   an loch mar sgàthan
na casan a' coiseachd air   gibht nan speur   a' lìonadh a thuigse
donn is òir-dhonn a' mhonaidh   latha foghair   sàmhach   falaichte

frasan ag uisgeachadh fonn   mìn-fhreastalach   feur ga dheothal
a' drùdhadh   do gach sgoltadh is sgàineadh   cùil is cealla
craobh nach do cheannaich   cuislean   an t-aineolach nach
   beannaich

O uisge   a ghiùlaineas làthach   poll agus salchar   's a thig glan
às a-rithist   aiseirigh an iongantais   dian nad bhrìgh   a ghiùlaineas
   fuil
gu cuislean a' chridhe   tobar a' ghliocais   Crìosda ar sìth.

Aon latha, bhrist an saoghal os-nàdarra air Daibhidh ...

20

Smaoinich e gun robh a h-uile nì nàdarrach,
mar a bha saidheans ga aithris,
a h-uile nì tro laghan àbhaisteach.

O, a Dhaibhidh, bu bheag do dhùil ris,
nad shuidhe san t-sèithear a' leughadh a' phàipeir –
casan air a' ghreabhal, soilleir, neo-mhùchte.

Chun an dorais, cha robh duine ann,
"Tha thu dol às do chiall", thuirt e ris fhèin
gus feasgar a chuala e srann

a' chait 's e coimhead ris an doras fhosgailte,
a' bhian a' seasamh air a cheann,
sgreuch às amhaich, a' cur fàilt' air an tosgaire

bho thìr nach b' aithne dha. Dha Daibhidh:
mar dà loidhne-stiuiridh air cairt-iùil
an t-seòladair, an dearbhadh os-nàdarra.

An saoghal àbhaisteach, adhbharan is buaidhean,
cha bhiodh e cho sìmplidh tuilleadh, mar Horatio,
tha barrachd ann na tha na bhruadair.

21

Na Ròpaichean

Thuirt an guth:
Seall os do chionn, am bearradh àrd sin,
sleamhainn, dubh a' cholas, gun ghrèim làimhe,
dìrich, faigh fios bho thar na h-oir as àirde.
Ciamar a dhìreas
mi gun ròpa?

Sgòr-bheinn smuain
e gun òrdugh.
Gabh an sùgan
seo de shràbhan;
bheir gaol nighneig
suas thu sàbhailt'.
Chaidh mi suas
an stalla gàbhaidh,
sràbh air sràbh
a' bleith san ànradh;
le buille thuit mi
sìos gu talamh,
brùite, goirt,
's gu tur falamh.
Seo dhut ròpa
ceart, naidhlan,
ùr, earbsach,
na dhèanamh daingeann;
smuaintean snìomhte
nach gabh innse,
laoich a shuain e,
gabh is sìn air.
Thug mi sùil
air àrd na carraig –
an dubh-chosnadh,
slighe chorrach;
corragan meilicht'
air cruas shnàthlan,
air chall an ceò
nan smuain neo-chràbhach;
Wittgentein
gam phutadh suas air;
basan gam feannadh
le cruas an fhuachd ud.

Strì is oidhirp,
òirleach 's òirleach –
's a' tuiteam rithist
air talamh gòrach.
Sùil ri binnean
àrd na clèite:
rathad dòlais
gun dòigh air èirigh;
ròp' is ròp
de dhiofar sheòrsa,
a' feuchainn suas
air aodann sgòr-bheinn,
a' dìreadh suas
le dòchas ro-mhath:
's a' tuiteam sìos
nam chlod, nas dorra.
Seall os do chionn gu àird a' bhearraidh,
creag na beatha gun tròcair, àird o nach do thill
an streapadair le fios cinnteach, le aon sealladh.

Ioanna anns na bliadhnaichean às dèidh na h-aisling a bhith aice ...

22

Aislingean a' tighinn 's a' falbh
ann an dùsal cadail – cho àbhaisteach –
air chuimhne, 's air dhòchuimhn' sa bhalbh
mhadainn, mar nach biodh iad ach
mar shradagan ag èirigh à teine,
aislingean ag aisling aisling,
gun bhrìgh. No an sealleadh eile,
iad nam pàirt den aisling fharsaing
a ghin am Facal aig tùs an latha,
uaireannan a' drùdhadh oirnn

le lùth neo-aithnicht', mar, iad 'g ràdh,
mise mìr den dealbh mhòr,
èist, èist ri mo theachdaireachd,
rim ghliocas dìomhair, ris an àm ri teachd.

23

Bha aisling aig Ioanna mar sin,
dhrùidh i oirre gu smior a cnàimh,
bliadhna às dèidh bliadhna ga leantainn,
ga stalcaireachd, gun fhaochadh, gun tàmh.
Carson mo smaoin air an duine ud
nach fhaca mi o chionn bliadhna nam bliadhn'?
Nam ònair a' sileadh dheòir, tha siud
gun chiall, cha robh mi mar seo riamh.
An àite bhith 'g ùrnaigh airson mo theaghlaich,
tha mi guidhe air a shon-san ri Dia.
Thalla! Thalla! Bha mi 'g ràdh 's teich,
ach chan fhalbhadh, 's bha mi a' triall
mar sin gus 'n do dh'inns mi do dhuine diadhaidh
a thuirt, Le dearbh chinnt 's ann bho Dhia i.

24

Ars an duine diadhaidh, Bha aisling
mar sin agamsa mus do choinnich mi
ri mo mhnaoi, 's às dèidh sin phòs sinn,
's thàinig faochadh gu Ioanna ri linn.
Dìomhair an nì, dìomhair an strì
tha fo uachdar an t-sruth dhaonnachdail,
gun fhios dhuinn tha fìor bhrìgh
ga dealbh 's gun sinn smaoineachadh.
'S ann bho mhullach na beinne a chì sinn
an rathad a' snàgadh shìos fodhainn,
gun for againn air an lùib gu h-ìseal

gun dèanamh i ciall air mullach romhainn.
Dha Ioanna, cha robh ciall san aisling,
ach doilgheas nach gabhadh aithris.

'S air eilean eile

25

Leis fhèin a' sireadh Dhè,
an e facal a bh' ann no fìrinn?
A ghlòir sgrìobht' air an speur,
ach reusan ga dhèanamh neo-chinnteach.
An creutair fa chomhair neo-chrìochnachd,
mar atam fa chomair na grèin';
math a dhèanamh mar fhiachan
air cridhe nach tuig e fhèin.

**Misneachd a-nise, innsidh i mun aisling dha banacharaid
Màiri. Gach bliadhna, bha iad a' dol gu Còmhdhail
Shoisgeulach san eilean san robh Daibhidh a' fuireach. Ma
bhruidhneas mi ris, smaoinich i, falbhaidh an t-uallach,
sguiridh am buaireadh. Fòn thuige, thuirt Màiri, fòn thuige.**

26

Tachraidh na rudan a thachras gun dùil
riutha, mar chloich a' ruith le bruthaich
sìos, le tuiteamas a' bualadh cùl
ulbhaig, 's a' dol air adhart gu suthach
gu cùil no còs eile gus mu dheireadh thall
a shleamhnicheas i gu fois ann an àite
nach deach a chur mu seach le càil,
shaoilte, ach turchairt nach robh na dhàn dhi.
Sin mar a bha inntinn Dhaibhidh mu chùisean,
nithean a' tachairt truimeach-air-shearrach

gun phlana daingeann a bhith gan stiùireadh,
clach na mì-riaghailt a' tuiteam seachad.
Gus an latha a thog e am fòn na làmh,
's cha bhiodh a bheatha gu bràth mar bha.

27

Halò, cò th' agam ann an seo? *Ioanna*,
thuirt an guth, nach fhada on uair sin,
halò, 's e Crìosdaidh a-nis a th' annam,
tha rud ann a tha gam bhuaireadh,
an tig thu chun a' phàillein a-màireach,
tha rud agam a dh'fheumas mi innse,
chan urrainn dhomh a ràdh an-dràsta
air a' fòn. A ghràidh ort , chaidh inntinn
Dhaibhidh air seachran seilge, air thuairmeas,
cha robh fhios aige dè thigeadh às a bheul,
an robh an tè seo ag iarraidh thighinn ga fhuasgladh
o bhruid a' pheacaidh an ainm Chrìosd'?
No, 'n e seo gu dearbh an sealgair naomh,
Is ise A shearbhant' son a thoirt gu saors'.

28

An Sealgair Naomh

od òige   bha mi gad dhian ruith   tarsaing bhoglaichean   sìos
   glòman
do-ruigsinn do dhaoine   thu falbh bhuam   mise gad shireadh   am poll
an clàbar do bheatha   thu diùltadh cuireadh às dèidh cuiridh   air
   falbh
bhuam   air do rathad fhèin   thu tionndadh air falbh   bhom ghunna
peilear a' ghaoil   a' feitheamh riut   airson do chridhe
   trobhad thuirt mi
uair às dèidh uair   tionndaidh d' aodann   ri fear do ghràidh

sìos monaidhean   suas beanntan   a-staigh dha na sgoran   a b'
iomallaiche

a' falach bhuam   gun ghuth agad   gu robh mi gad fhaicinn   cho
faisg ort

ri do chraiceann   ach gam àicheadh   turas is turas   dha na h-
àiteachadh gàbhaidh

silteach   bàthte   dhan aigeann fhèin   dhan dubh-aigeann

lean mi thu   le mo ghunna   's do shùilean làn eagail   teich thuirt
thu

teich bhuam   chan eil mi ag iarraidh   a bhith cràbhach   tha mi ro
òg

airson do ghràdh-sa   cha ghabhadh tu làmh   a shaoradh tu   bho
na sluganan craosach

ach lean mi   lean mi thu   a dh'aindeoin claisean   is bruthaichean
do bhrosnachaidh

tionndaidh   tionndaidh thuirt mi   d' aodann rium   agus gheibh
thu

peilear a' ghaoil   na do chridhe   is mise an sealgair naomh   nach
gabh diùltadh

tha saorsa agad   tionndadh rium   air an lorg shìorraidh   ruigidh
mo ghaol-sa

an t-sloc gun ìochdar   gabh ris   gabh ri mo ghunna   gabh ri mo
pheilear

agus anns an dùnadh   chì thu an fhìrinn   chì thu mise   fear do
ghràidh

tha do shaorsa agad   chan èignich mi   gu bràth thu   ach
tionndaidh   tionndaidh d' aodann

29

Is fiadh-bheathach an cridhe,
's is doirbh e a cheann'sadh,
an inntinn a' frithealadh
targaidean (a) annsachd;

smaointean a' leantainn
air earball na bèiste –
cridhe is eanchainn
san eabar le chèile.

30

Sa Phàillean

Thuirt Daibhidh ri Ioanna gun tigeadh e 's dòcha gu coinneamh a'
    phàillein
's bha ise 's a banacharaid nan suidhe ag èisteachd ri brìgh na
    teachdaireachd
ach cha robh esan ann, cha robh sgeul air an deamhain, *Cuir fòn*
    thuige,
thuirt Màiri , *Cha chuir gu dearbh ged a bhocadh e, thuirt ise, cha*
    chuir.
'S dìreach mar a thuirt i na facail thàinig facail eile à beul an
    teachdaire,
Cha las duine coinneal airson a cur fo shoitheach, thalla, Ioanna,
    thalla!
Chaidh saighead tro a feòil, phut na facail i, phut Màiri, phut Dia i,
's gun fhios aig an teachdaire air càil dhe na bha tachairt, thàinig a
    chomhairle
's ghabh ise a chomhairle is dh'fhòn i a-rithist ged nach b' ann gun nàire,
dh'fhòn i 's dh'aontaich iad gun coinnicheadh iad an àite eile a-
    màireach.

31

Anns a' Chafaidh

Mar theicheas tìm, mar a dh'atharraicheas aodainn,
mu dheireadh iad nan suidhe a' gabhail beachd air a chèile;
iomadh uisge agus tuil air sruthadh gun fhaochadh,
faileas san aghaidh dhen duine a bh' ann, air èiginn

ag aithneachadh a chèile, a' cuimhneachadh nan slighean
a ghabh iad o chionn sia bliadhna deug thar fhichead;
pòsadh is dealachadh, gun dòigh ac' air a thighinn
còmhla gus a' mhionaid seo. An òige nan sligean.

Dh'inns i a h-uallach, mar a bha an aisling ga buaireadh,
's nan innseadh i dha gum faigheadh i faochadh,
bha i 'n dòchas. 'S e sin a thuirt i an uair sin
's esan a' smaointinn, An tàinig an tè seo gam shaoradh?

'S beag a dh'fhios dhi air anam, na ceuman tulgach,
na creagan cas, dubh-shlocan an uabhais,
an sireadh 's an claonadh, na frith-rathaidean cealgach,
tro smaoin a' lorg aonadh, e fhèin làn buairidh.

Ach dhealaich iad 's dh'fhalbh iad 's ghal i sa chàr,
toilichte, thuirt e, ach cha robh sin na shùilean.
's beag a dh'fhios an coinnicheadh iad rithist gu bràth,
ach a-nis i 'n dòchas gum biodh i saor 's gun chùram.

32

Dh'fhairich Daibhidh an sealgair a-nis aig a shàilean,
an sealgair naomh nach b' urrainn dha àicheadh.

33

An Cafaidh Maireannach

Tha cofaidh a' ghràis ann
is uachdar a' mhaitheanais,
is gràdh an t-siùcair 's mìlse
toirt an cìs gach faireachadh.

Ann an rìoghachd a' chridhe,
tha an cafaidh maireannach;
anns a' choille mhòr ud
gheibhear teach a' charthannais.

Air taobh thall smuain,
ann an dùthaich an fhaireachaidh,
theirig slighe tron choill,
's dòch' gun dèan thu aithneachadh.

Mar a thachair do Dhaibhidh
aon lath 's e air allaban
anns a' choille mhòir sin
is cùisean air fairtleachadh.

Dh'fhairich e blàths a' tighinn
bho àirde nach do dh'aithnich e;
cha robh fhios cò às a bha e,
ach *bha* e ga tharraing thuig'.

Thuig e nach robh sa bhàidh ud
ach blàths a' ghràidh mhaireannaich:
cha dhìochuimhnich e an tlàths ud
fhad 's is beò air thalamh e.

Cha robh e mar nì saoghalta,
ach bha e bàidheil carthannach,
cho saor ri gaoth nam beanntan
mar theine tìorail tarraingeach.

Is fada, fada thall e,
ach cho faisg oirnn ri faireachadh,
a' ceangal tìm is biothbhuantachd
tha cafaidh còir a' charthannais.

'S ann an rìoghachd a' chridhe
a tha 'n taigh-bìdh maireannach:
ma gheibh sinn uair na lùib,
a chaoidh cha bhi sinn dealaichte.

34

Ach cha do sguir am buaireadh.
Uair no dhà choinnich iad,
gheibh mi bradan fiadhaich,
smaoinich i, mus tèid mi ga fhaicinn.
Leth-uair a thìde, 's gun dùil ris,
fònaidh tè a dh'aithnicheas i
air tilleadh à Leòdhas,
A bheil thu 'g iarraidh bradan fiadhaich,
thuirt i, *tha cus an seo dhuinne.*
Thèid seachd mìosan seachad,
fònaidh esan. *Tha mi dìreach air cairt*
a chuir sa phost, thuirt i.
Làrna-mhàireach thàinig an cairt.
Co-thuiteamasan gun chrìch,
mar gum biodh lamh neo-fhaicsinneach
gan stiùireadh còmhla.
Ann am bliadhna bha iad pòsta.

35

Air an latha thuit am maide
bhon tarraig 's gun duine dlùth;
bu mhòr an imcheist air inntinn
Dhaibhidh – doirbh dian a' chùis.

Gach nì nàdarrach na riaghailt,
sin bha e den làn bheachd uair:
cha ghluais nì sam bith gun adhbhar,
no bidh ar beatha gun stuaim.

Chan ann aon uair ach còig uairean
a ghluais am maide gu làr;
mar gum biodh e ag ràdh riutha,
sgrìobh an leabhar sin gun dàil,

an leabhar a bha e sgrìobhadh,
sgeul an slighe ceum air cheum,
mar a rinn an Triath a shaoradh
às an t-sloc uamhraidh is breun.

'S thachair ceud nì eile riutha,
air nach robh mìneachadh luath,
cinnteachadh bho shaoghal thairis
gu bheil aig an Spiorad buaidh.

E nis a' creidsinn na Fìrinn,
mu dheireadh, mu dheireadh thall,
gur e Dia, Crìosda 's an Spiorad
an Triùir as fiùghanta th' ann.

Saoghal gun chiall is gun adhbhar,
no le doimhneachdan gun ghrunnd,
a' tighinn bho Chuspair sìorraidh
's an Crìosda a thug e dhuinn.

**Tha Daibhidh a' smaoineachadh air an Aiseirigh mar nì
eachdraidheil a thachair ...**

36

Air Rathad Emàuis

1

Ar cinn sìos, ceuman neo-èasgaidh,
's Ierusalem air ar cùlaibh;
dust an rathaid, teas na grèine
's a h-uile nì na bhriseadh dùile.

Esan a bha dol gar saoradh,
dh'fhàg sinn e air a' chrann-ceusaidh;

a bha gu bhith na rìgh Israeil,
e air cùl carraig gun èirigh.

Aisling eile, nach e, dìreach
aisling, thèid sinn gu Emàus
gu ar càirdean 's gun ri innse
ach an sgeul bhrònach chràidhteach,

sinne a' sùileachadh Messiah,
mar a gheall e a's na fàidhean,
nis gun dòchas gum bi rìoghachd
Israeil a chaoidh na sealbh dhuinn.

Tha mo chridhe, a Chleòpais,
dìreach cho sgìth, gu toirt thairis,
smaointinn mar a bha e a' fulang
's na daoine bha siud a' fanaid.

2

Cò e, cò e tha a' tighinn air ar cùlaibh?
Na ceuman, a bheil thu gan cluinntinn,
aotrom, ealamh gun chùram?

Neach-turais le cleòca mu cheann,
còmhla rinn a' coiseachd,
a Chleòpais, cò idir a th' ann?

Chan eil fhios, ach tha e fiosrach dha-rìribh
san sgriobtar, gun teagamh,
ach nach neònach na tha e 'g innse,

gum feum am fàidh bhith air a cheusadh
air taobh a-muigh a' bhaile
's às dèidh trì latha gum bi e 'g èirigh

's nach bi èis na bheatha tuilleadh
ach gum bi e na rìgh air an t-saoghal
gus am bi crìoch air na h-uile.

Cò e, cò e? Tha mo chridhe losgadh annam
ag èisteachd ris air an t-slighe,
nach ann ann a tha an co-chomann.

Tha an dorchadas a' tighinn,
nach fan thu còmhla rinn gu madainn?
Chan eil fad' againn ri dhol a-nise.

3

Thàinig e staigh, thàinig e staigh, thàinig e staigh do ar dachaigh,
thàinig sinn còmhla mun a' bhòrd agus bhrist e an t-aran.
A Dhè nan gràs, shoillsich solas, 's e esan bh' ann, chan eil dol às air,
esan, Ìosa, ar caraid, esan bh' ann, tha e beò air an talamh,
tha e air èirigh o na mairbh, chan eil fhios ciamar a thachair
leithid de nì, ach tha e dearbhte, bha e seo fo ar cabair.
A Chleòpais, mìorbhail, iongantas, tròcair nach gabh aithris,
bha am Mesias an seo, mu ar coinneamh, na nì aithnicht',
dìreach mar a smaoinich sinn gur robh e uile seachad,
Ìosa na ghlòir an seo, 's an uair sin chaidh e à sealladh.
Feumaidh sinn a dhol a' chiad char sa mhadainn,
gu Ierusalem, gus an inns sinn, chan fhaigh mi srad cadail.

37

A' bhuil

Seo an t-ugh
a thug thu dhomh
ri taobh na h-aibhne
an latha ud sna Islands,

ugh na Càisge,
soilleir, làn dhathan,
ged nach robh mi faicinn
dad dheth an lath' ud.

Seo an geata
a chunnaic mi san aisling;
seo an Cuspair
a bha gar tarraing.

Seo na cluaintean uaine
a bhiadhas an cridhe,
's gun fhios dhuinn, gar stiùireadh,
aodhair na slighe.

Seo do 'dhùbhlan'
air a fhreagairt;
do theagamhan nam bruan,
's do chion creideimh.

Spealgan fiodha
do bheatha
dol eagarra còmhla
mar bhùird eathair.

38

Gun tigeadh do Rìoghachd

Tha do rìoghachd làn de ghlòir
a' soillseachadh nan cùiltean dorch',
mar bhith dùsgadh à cadal suain,
a' tuigsinn gu bheil rìoghachd annainn bhuat.

A' dùsgadh mar bho aisling bheò,
an 'solas' ud a-nis na sgleò,
a' bheatha a bh' ann na bruadar,
sinn nad chomann gràidh 's coluadair;

Thu dùsgadh annam smuaintean dìomhair,
do Spiorad gam tharraing gu d' iarraidh,
an sgàile naomh fo fheòil an t-saoghail
a' lasadh suas gach mìr der n-aonadh.

Dealan-dè bhon chochall bhrataig
ag èirigh dhan speur gu tapaidh,
a' fàgail na cuibhrichean prìosain
's a' dealradh le dathan prìseil.

Do rìoghachd na h-aiseirigh bheò
sa chridhe tha creidsinn do ghlòir;
sgàilean an aineolais a' sgapadh,
mathanas an dèidh deòir aidmheil.

Gun tigeadh do rìoghachd air talamh,
gun soillsicheadh i gach annam,
spiorad a charthannais a' lìonadh
gach cridhe led ghràs gun chrìonadh.

The Promised Land

A Poem Sequence

Maoilios Caimbeul

David and Joanna married in middle age. They first met when she was 17 and he was 19, but they went their different ways and didn't meet again for 36 years. A dream Joanna had was what led them to meet again and to marry. Joanna believed the dream was from God. Years after getting married, they were talking about writing a book about what had happened to them. David was doubtful about matters of faith and that supernatural events could take place. Until one day, after being married for 6 years …

1

It was a normal day,
the day the stick fell;
they were sitting at their meal
in the kitchen and he said to her –
Perhaps we should write the book.
Perhaps, she said, *perhaps we should.*
And the stick fell.

It shouldn't have fallen, it was only a stick,
a lifeless stick, without breath or energy or awareness.
It was a long stick for opening the loft door
and it hung on a nail in the hallway,
for years,
and it fell with a clatter to the floor,
it fell on its own with no-one near it.

It fell when David said to his wife,
Perhaps we ought to write the book,
the book about their life they were thinking of writing,
It would tell of God's dealings with them,
how they met after many long years
because of Joanna's dream.

O, Joanna, why did you have that dream,
why did it torment you, the pain and tears
for a person you hadn't seen
for thirty-six years?
Why did the preacher say to you?
It's from God. I had the same kind of dream
before I met my wife.

They were sitting at the table when the stick fell;
they got a huge surprise when it fell
with no-one near it.
(There on the nail for sixteen years,
without falling.)

David wasn't happy.
Deep thoughts darkened his heart.
Is it a premonition asking me
to empty the loft?
To cart off the clutter of years.
Is this the end?
It shouldn't happen, a stick falling on its own,
with no-one near it, with not a breath of wind.

On that day, their world changed.
The sky, and the book,
was another colour.

A week after that
going on to midnight
as they were falling asleep

they heard the clatter in the hall.
The stick had fallen again.

God of grace, save us.

Next day, he started
emptying the loft.

And he sat at his desk, writing.

Remembering the old days ...

2

Do you remember when we met
in Inverness that spring?
You gave me a chocolate Easter egg.
I remember, you were seventeen,
in your green corduroy coat,
under the trees in The Islands
and you were surprised that I gave you an egg.
It surprised me too that I gave you an egg,
a beautiful coloured silvery egg.
But nothing living came from it,
you left me for someone else,
back to your first love
and you married and had children
and I went the way of the prodigal son.

3

Before it, he was young in loving spaces.
Before it, she was young in loving spaces.
Godly parents plying them with health,
but to them, freedom-denying shackles,
half alive in the isles of bondage,
release me, let me go, was their cry.

4

Who is this?

The little Skye boy
deep in books,
mind flying with 'if' and 'but';

a complete Gaelic world
but sepsis at its heart,
school the pernicious boil.

But who is this offering wisdom,
with scarlet books at the door,
an encyclopaedia from Newnes?

The little boy with the new Bible
imbibed like milk and porridge,
Darwin and Freud the dear purchase.

The black book and the red,
blood in the soil of ages,
and the cross becomes the tree of wrath.

5

As regards him

in the far-off land
among the pigs
fed with the crumbs
and husks of lust

the years pass

the parched desert
shooting stars
countless thoughts
falling in the darkness

the years pass

falling in the dismal
sky of despair
nothingness, edge
of horror and dread

who created the mountains?

one of ordinance absolute –
Him far from his thought,
but in the hidden soil
unknown to him the seed was growing

and the years pass

6

I remembered you
although I ignored you –
in a despised recess
of my mind you were there
along with the others.

7

As regards her

house and family
alien streets
and human love
and the odd party

Joseph far from his people

island visitors
brothers, sisters,

preparing food
and God on the shelf

Joseph regretting his bondage

8

I didn't remember you
but like yourself
in a hidden recess –
my life was filled
with mundane work.

9

Him

He dreams poems, entangled in thought,
climbing the mountain and finding nothing
but junk of reason that couldn't satisfy the heart,

these white mountains before him
and O, aye, the crystal lakes on the summits,
but, on arrival, dryness and drought.

Tell me you're there, he would say,
above the white, the birds and desire,
and he would go home with a bad taste in his mouth.

He would hunt the white hind
and it would go clean from his sight
on the ridge as if it had never been there.

On a day he stood before the nothingness
and with a challenge said, prove to me
that you exist, go on prove it;

nothing but the heights of provocation,
but he looked down and there on the table
the words written on an ashtray

'The Challenge.'

**After years in the city, Joanna returned to where she was
born and brought up ...**

10

While he dreamed poems, she dreamed of returning
from the crowded city to her island, the source
of her hope, Joseph returning at last
from the far country, laden with wealth.

Over there, her father and brothers wait.
She also climbed mountains and moors
full of bogs, caves and pits on the way
unable to stand in sludge and mire.

Wanting nothing to do with church – doleful
images, stern shrouds of authority –
don't cut your hair, don't show love at church door –
surface rules, avoiding the hidden.

In a sky she hoped would be blue,
black, ruthless clouds rose on the horizon,
tempestuous winds hurling her
like a paper boat torn apart.

She held her father to her breast in his dying,
her Jacob who she loved so much,
carried with the stream in the chaos of the sea,
herself caught up in the swelling anguish.

In extremity of soul, trembling with dread,
in her crisis she opened the book and read:
Be still and know that I am God. And instantly,
her body was still and her soul was at peace.

The burdens of the years dispelled and she said:
Such knowledge is
too wonderful for me,
too lofty for me to attain.

And at last when she went to church –
despite that body's shortcomings –
it was as if he was reading her thoughts,
the sermon attending to her every need.

**For years, David was lost among philosophies and religions,
searching and not finding ...**

11

Him and the Voice

Pensively I walk
on the shell shards of the heart,
soles cut up
and bleeding.
The voice said, I couldn't care less,
it's your very own fault,
didn't your father tell you before you left,
Trust in God, and good will follow you.

But you took the hill and shore road,
the stray mean way. You trampled
the holy flowers under your feet,
and drank from the bitter foul bogs of your desire.

Reason broke my faith,
everything was natural;
sea breaking pitilessly on shore,
the innocent dispatched without a tear.

Don't put your trust in the shore
or in the surface of the sea;
your learning will take long but you'll reach
to the depth in the day of mercy.

When the moon is full
above the ocean, in the eternal scale,
you will see the whole picture,
and all things complete.

12

The Faces

He walked in the wood
faces shone above him
in the ancient clear light

the lunar faces he didn't understand
seeking and visiting him
from the unreachable distant kingdom

the minister on Hope Street –
he was in Glasgow with his father –
a face full of grace and happiness,

a glimpse from a region he doesn't understand,
and always his mother's face
an eternal question he cannot fathom

and the young lady with tinge
of the transcendent in her face
as if she had always been flower

and the wife near to death
with inscrutable peace in her eyes,
although she knew well what was coming

and the image of his father in the coffin
as if he had just met
with the creator unawares.

Faces haunt him, lunar faces,
struck by glimmers of grace,
torment him, and disappear.

13

Because eternity can break through time,
and because it is inherent in the heart,
because the face is in and out of time,
look at it closely when you speak to her.

Look at his face when you speak to him,
pose yourself the questions, don't postpone:
In this inter-face, who is speaking to me?
Whose is the light revealing laughter?

From where came the rose blessing the air?
The 'I' and the 'you' are like questions for each of us.
A sacred spirit plays in your eyes,
not love but the depth of creation I read.

After years on her native island, Joanna left for England ...

14

I'm tired of this,
I'm sick with it,
it's really choking me –
and she saw the shoreline through her tears.

She came there gladly
and she left it sadly:
pain in the parting
and waves of confusion.

Island of her tears,
and of her comfort
seeing it on the horizon
as the boat sailed,

as her soul sailed
to another country
and she could see Canaan behind her
and the Egypt of her sorrow.

In Cranleigh in Surrey,
away from rancour,
serving the old folk,
God's peace and quiet.

15

The years pass,
peace and anguish, in the end,
and she returned again, a widow,
to the isle of her birth and upbringing.
Her brother gave her the family home
and she started mending it.

God of mercy
keep me sane;
the road is difficult
and sharp your sword,
but also
words of comfort
stream from your mouth.

My heart
within me
is full of gladness
at your story,
my soul sings
a new song
like the lark on high.
O, my soul sings
a new song
like the lark in the sky

16

On that night I had the dream,
I went to bed sorrowful,
an argument with the builder
throwing me off course.

God, why me, why,
why do the waves break on me?
Why does this world
leave me a poor soul?

Tears and unsettled sleep,
my life flaying me,
when I wakened from the dream
from which I didn't want to wake.

A grey-haired man
signalling me to follow him
through a gate to a green field
to where there would be peace and happiness.

When he turned to face me,
I saw David's face,
older, but it was him
giving me his hand.

Sweet the peace, smooth the field,
green trees on each side;
God, don't let me waken,
leave me in this sleep.

But I wakened to the world of worry,
to a house needing repaired:
little did I know the coming struggle,
how the dream would refuse to go away.

17

Echoes in the mind, Stalin, Pol Pot,
murder, killing and every rotten thing,

hellish names screaming -
Biafra, Israel and Egypt,

Khmer Rouge, Burundi, Indonesia,
death and civil massacre

unnamed millions in the earth
in a hopeless war not vetoed.

What kind of creature are we,
living of fellow creatures' flesh and oaths?

Rwanda, Congo and the rest,
like a nasty smell in our nostrils

red foliage on the world's fields,
senseless destruction without respite.

18

The soft voice said in his ear, Couldn't it be different? –
'Father, forgive them, for they don't know what they do' –
Couldn't it be like the bird nesting the brood, the chicks
hidden under wing, safe, love giving them security?

Care instead of blade, peace instead of blood-soaked earth,
unity, not separation. Nurture the innocent to old age
in the house of fellowship. We are all of the same soul,
the one root, the angel and devil inhabiting all.

The soft voice said in his ear, Couldn't it be different,
humanity matured, the rose sporting with the thorn,
the society of the rose making the earth fragrant
and the spirit of peace ruling underdog and mighty.

19

The Miracle of water

O yes   he saw the water   amazing
in the dawn of the world   miracle born
streaming from the hidden   soft   transparency

covering the world   the radiant canopy
still as a mirror   next minute   a roaring beast
depths   chambers full of life   fish-caressed

winter morning   crystal patterns   on glass and pool
delicate fingers   intricate designs   transient embroidery
real instant art   certain   certain   as the temperature

water   your story is true   velvet soft   kind
and hard   you break the rock   eroding its goodness
to streams and rivers   carrying the mud of life   to level plain

your story is true   the carrying substance   meaning-full
whisperer to rock   your way is music to the thirsty   great
your melodious friendship with the wildernesses   perfect harmony

yes   he saw the water   the loch like a mirror
feet walking on it   sky's gift   filling his sense
moor's brown and golden-brown   autumn day   silent   hidden

showers watering land   fine provision   grass-sipped
penetrating   to every crack and cranny   nook and cell
by tree unbought   arteries   by the blind unblessed

water!   carrying mire   mud and dirt   to come clean
again   reborn wonder   intense in essence   carrier of blood
to heart veins   wisdom well   Christ our peace.

One day, the supernatural world broke in on David ...

20

He thought everything was natural,
as science reported it,
everything through natural law.

Ah, David, you little expected it,
sitting in your chair reading the paper –
footsteps on the gravel, clear, unmuffled.

To the door, nobody there,
you're going mad, he said to himself
until in the afternoon he heard the wail

of the cat as it faced the open door,
its fur standing on end,
a shriek from its throat, welcoming the ambassador

from a land it didn't know. For David:
like two bearings on a sailor's
chart, the supernatural proof.

The normal world, causes and effects,
it wouldn't be as simple any more, like Horatio,
there was more to it than *his* vision.

21

The Ropes

The voice said:
Look above you, that high escarpment,
slippery, dark looking, without handhold,
climb, ascertain what's beyond the highest edge.
How can I ascend
without a rope?
The disorderly
high cliff of thought.
Take this twisted
straw rope;
a girl's love will
take you safely.
I went up
the perilous cliff face,
straw by straw
eroding in the stress;
with a thud I fell
down to earth,
bruised, sore,
and completely empty.
Here is a proper rope
for you, nylon,
new, trustworthy,
strongly made;
entwined thoughts
untold,
warriors wound it,
take and lean on it.
I had a look
at the high crag –
a hard slog,

uneven way;
frozen fingers
on the hard strands,
lost in mist
of unholy thoughts;
Wittgenstein
pushing me upwards;
palms flayed
by the callous cold.
Striving and struggle,
inch by inch –
and falling again
to a senseless earth.
I look at the high
point of the outcrop:
a dismal path
with no ascent;
rope after rope
of different kinds,
attempting to climb
the mountain cliff,
climbing upwards
full of hope:
and falling down
in a heap, more taxed.
Look above you to the summit of the ridge,
merciless is life's cliff, a height from which no climber
has returned with certain knowledge, with one view.

Joanna in the years after the dream ...

22

Dreams come and go
in drowsy sleep – so natural –

remembered, and forgotten in the still
morning, as if they were but
sparks rising from a fire,
dreams dreaming dreams,
senseless. Or the other view,
they as part of a wider dream
born of the Word in time's dawn,
sometimes affecting us
with unknown power, as if saying,
I'm a fragment of the great picture,
listen, listen to my message,
to my mysterious wisdom, to future time.

23

Joanna had such a dream,
it penetrated to her marrow
year after year following her,
stalking her, ceaseless, without respite.
Why do I think of that man
who I haven't seen since whenever?
Crying on my own, it's
just senseless, I was never like this.
Instead of praying for my family,
I'm pleading to God for him.
Go! Go! I would say, get,
but it wouldn't, and so I went on
like that until I told a holy man
who said, Certainly, it is from God.

24

Said the holy man, I had a similar
dream once before I met
my wife, and afterwards we married,
and as a result Joanna was relieved.

It is hidden, mysterious the striving,
under the surface of the human stream,
without our knowledge a true meaning
is unconsciously being devised.
It's from the mountaintop we see
the road meandering below us,
with no idea that the bend beneath
would make sense when we reach the summit.
For Joanna, the dream had no meaning,
but vexation she couldn't begin to tell.

And on another island ...

25

By himself seeking God,
was it merely a word or truth?
His glory written on the skies,
but reason making it uncertain.
The creature in the face of the eternal,
like an atom before the sun;
to do good a duty on a heart
that doesn't understand itself.

**Having confidence now, she tells her friend Mary about
the dream. Every year, they would go to a gospel event on
the island where David was staying. If I speak to him, she
thought, the burden will go, the worry will stop. Phone him,
Mary said, phone him.**

26

Things that happen happen
unexpectedly, like a stone rolling down
a slope, by chance striking the back

of a boulder, and going merrily on
to a recess or other hollow until at last
it slides to a stop in some place
that wasn't set aside for it by anything,
apparently, but a fluke not set by fate.
That's how David thought of events,
things happening topsy-turvy
without an overarching plan guiding them,
the unruly stone falling past.
Until the day he lifted the phone in his hand,
and his life would never again be the same.

27

Hello, who do I have here? *Joanna,*
the voice said, it's been a long time,
Hello, I'm a Christian now,
there's something that's bothering me,
can you come to the tent tomorrow,
there's something I must tell you,
I can't tell you now on the
phone. O dear, David's mind
drifted, at random,
he didn't know what to say,
did this person want his release
from the captivity of sin in Christ's name?
Or, was this indeed the holy hunter,
and her His servant to bring him to freedom.

28

The Holy Hunter

from your youth   I hotly pursued you   across morasses   down
   chasms

inaccessible to man   running from me   as I went after   in the mud
and mire of your life   refusing invitation   after invitation   going
from me   on your own way   turning from me   from my gun
the bullet of love   waiting for you   for your heart   come I said
time after time   turn you face   to your love

down moor lands   up mountains   into the clefts   most distant
hiding from me   ignoring   that I was seeing you   as near to you
as your skin   but denying me   time after time   to the dangerous
   places
soaking   drowning   to the abyss itself   to the deepest abyss
I followed you   with my gun   and your eyes full of fear   go away you
   said
go away from me   I don't want you   to be pious   I'm too young

for your love   you wouldn't accept a hand   to free you   from the
   gaping ravines
but I followed   I followed you   despite ditches   and the hills   of your
   incitement
turn   turn I said   your face to me   and you will get
the bullet of love   in your heart   I am the holy hunter   one cannot
   refuse
you have freedom   turn to me   on the eternal path   my love will
   reach
the bottomless pit   accept it   accept my gun   accept my bullet

and in the end   you'll see the truth   you'll see me   your desired one
you have your freedom   I will not force you   ever   but turn   turn
   your face

29

The heart is a wild animal,
and difficult to subdue,
the mind attends
the targets of its desire;

thoughts follow
on the tail of the beast –
heart and mind
in the mire together.

30

In the Tent

David told Joanna that he might come to the meeting in the tent,
and she and her friend sat listening to the meaning of the message,
but he wasn't there, no sign of the devil, *phone him*
Mary said, *No indeed, though he would jump, she said, not at all.*
And just as she said the words the preacher spoke these,
No-one lights a candle to put under a dish, go, Joanna, go!
Her body was stung, the words impelled her, Mary impelled her, God
    impelled her,
completely unaware of what was happening the preacher's advice
    came
and she took his advice and phoned again, although embarrassed,
she phoned and they agreed to meet somewhere else next day.

31

In the Café

How time flies, how faces change,
sitting at last taking stock of each other;
water and flood have streamed without respite,
in the face is shadow of former self, hardly

recognising each other, remembering the ways
they journeyed through thirty-six years;
marriage and parting, with no means
of meeting until this moment. Their youth in shards.

She told him her worry, how she was troubled by the dream,
and, if she told him, how she would get relief,
she hoped. That's what she said at the time,
as he thought, Did this person come to free me?

Little did she know his mind, the faltering steps,
the precipitous cliffs, the dark hellish pits,
the seeking and misdirection, the deceitful pathways,
through thought searching for unity, himself full of unease.

But they parted and she went and cried in the car,
happy, he said, but it didn't show in his eyes,
who knows if they would ever meet again,
but now she hoped she would be free from care.

32

Now David felt the hunter at his heels,
the holy hunter who he couldn't deny.

33

The everlasting café

It has the coffee of grace
and the cream of forgiveness,
and love, the sweetest sugar,
ruling all feeling.

In the country of the heart
is the everlasting café;
in that great forest
you will find the love's locus.

On the other side of thought,
in the land of feeling,
take the road through the wood,
perhaps you'll recognise it.

As happened to David
one day in his wanderings
in the great forest
when things had failed for him.

He felt a warmth coming
from a region unknown;
he didn't know where it came from,
but he *was* drawn to it.

He understood the affection
as the warmth of everlasting love:
he will never forget its tenderness
as long as he lives.

It wasn't of this world,
but it was gentle and loving,
as free as the mountain air
like a homely alluring fire.

It's far, far away,
but as near to us as feeling,
binding time and eternity
is the kindly love café.

The everlasting café
is in the kingdom of the heart:
if we ever come into it,
we will never be estranged.

34

The trouble and worry didn't stop.
Once or twice they met,
I'll get a wild salmon,
she thought, before I go and see him.
Half an hour later, unexpectedly,

an acquaintance phones
just returned from Lewis,
Do you want a piece of wild salmon,
she said, *there's too much for us.*
Seven months pass,
he phones. *I've just sent
you a postcard*, she said.
Next day he got the card.
Endless coincidences,
as if an invisible hand
was bringing them together.
Within a year they were married.

35

The day the stick fell
from the nail with no-one near;
David was bewildered –
matters were difficult, severe.

Everything according to natural law,
that's how he thought once:
nothing moves without a cause,
or our lives will be a mess.

Not once but five times,
the stick fell to the floor;
as if it was saying to them,
go ahead and write this book,

the book he was writing,
their life's story step by step,
how the Triune saved him
from the hideous slimy pit.

And a hundred other things happened to them,
with no easy explanation,
demonstration from a world beyond
of the power of the Spirit.

He now believed the Truth,
at last, at long last,
that God, Christ and the Spirit
are the three most worthy.

A world without sense and cause,
or with unfathomable depth,
come from an eternal Subject
and the Christ he gave us.

David thinks of the Resurrection as something historical that took place ...

36

On the Road to Emmaus

1

Our heads bowed, feet dragging,
Jerusalem behind us;
the dust of the road, heat of the sun
and everything a disappointment.

He who was going to save us,
we left him on the cross;
who was going to be the king of Israel,
buried behind a boulder.

Another dream, isn't it, just
a dream, we'll go to Emmaus

to our relatives with nothing to tell
but the sorrowful painful story,

expecting a Messiah,
as promised by the prophets,
now without hope that Israel
will ever have its kingdom.

My heart, Cleopas,
is just so tired, almost giving up,
thinking of how he suffered
and these people mocking him.

2

Who is it, who is it coming behind us?
The steps, do you hear the steps,
light, swift and easy?

A visitor with cloak on his head,
walking along with us,
Cleopas, who on earth is it?

No idea, but without doubt
he knows the scriptures well,
but isn't it strange what he tells us,

that the prophet must be crucified
outside the city walls
and after three days he will rise

and his life will lack nothing
but he will be king of the world
until the end of time.

Who is he, who is he? My heart burns in me
listening to him in the way,
what company he is.

It's getting dark,
won't you stay with us till morning?
We haven't got far to go now.

3

He came in, he came in to our home,
we came together at the table and he broke bread.
O gracious God, a light shone, it was him, no doubt about it,
him, Jesus, our friend, it was him, he is alive on earth,
he has risen from the dead, who knows how such a thing
could have happened, but it's proven, he was under our roof.
O Cleopas, a miracle, a wonder, a mercy beyond speech,
the Messiah was here, before us, fully known,
just as we thought that it was all over,
Jesus here in his glory and then he disappeared.
We must be off first thing in the morning,
to Jerusalem, until we tell, I won't get a wink of sleep.

37

The Result

This is the egg
you gave me
beside the river
that day in The Islands

the Easter egg,
bright, full of colours,
although I didn't see
any of that then.

This is the gate
I saw in the dream;
this is the Subject
who was drawing us.

These are the green fields
to feed the heart,
and unknown to us, guiding us,
the shepherd of the way.

Here is your 'challenge'
answered;
your doubts in smithereens,
and your lack of faith.

The wood splinters
of your life
fitting exactly together
as the boards of a boat.

38

Your Kingdom Come

Your Kingdom is full of glory
lighting up the dark recesses,
as if wakening from a deep sleep,
understanding there is a kingdom within us from you.

As if wakening from a living dream,
the 'light' now is become a shadow,
the life that was a delusion,
existing in your communion of love and fellowship;

You waken hidden thoughts in me,
your Spirit draws me to seek you,
the holy shadow beneath fleshed out world
lights up the least fragment of our union.

Butterfly from a caterpillar pupa
rises strongly in the air,
leaves the prison bonds
and glitters with finest colours.

Your Kingdom a living resurrection
in the heart that believes your glory;
the veils of ignorance flee,
forgiveness after tears of confession.

Your Kingdom come on earth,
may it lighten every soul,
the spirit of charity filling
every heart with your unreserved grace.

Notes

Biblical references are to the NIV unless otherwise stated.

Chapter 1

1. Psalm, 105.17

Chapter 2

1. Caimbeul, M., *Eileanan*, (Department of Celtic, University of Glasgow, 1980), 30 (translated)
2. Magee, Bryan, *The Story of Philosophy*, (Dorling Kindersley, 1998), 172
3. ibid, 174

Chapter 4

1. Caimbeul, M., 'Silent Moon', *Bailtean*, (Gairm, 1987), 29
2. Caimbeul, M., 'Sùil air Ais', *A' Càradh an Rathaid*, (Coiscéim, 1988), 20–22
3. Schaeffer, Francis A., *Escape from Reason*, (Inter-varsity Fellowship, 1968), 36
4. ibid, 53
5. ibid, 48
6. Cupitt, Don, *The Sea of Faith, Christianity in Change*, (BBC, 1984), 247
7. ibid, 248
8. ibid, 269
9. Schaeffer, Francis A., *The God Who is There*, (Hodder & Stoughton, 1968), 78
10. *A' Gabhail Ris*, (Gairm, Glasgow, 1994), 12
11. ibid, 14
12. ibid, 15–16

Chapter 6

1. Jung, C. G., Memories, Dreams, Reflections, (Collins and Routledge & Kegan Paul, 1963), 136
2. Jung, C. G. *Selected Writings*, (Fontana Press, 1986), 16
3. Caimbeul, M., *A' Càradh an Rathaid*, (Coiscéim, Dublin, 1988), 94–96
4. ibid, 96
5. Jung, C. G., Selected Writings, (Fontana Press, 1986), 26
6. The Oxford Companion to Philosophy, Ted Honerich ed. (Oxford University Press, 1995), 436
7., 8. & 9., ibid, 436
10. Küng, Hans, *Does God Exist?* Collins & Doubleday, 1980), 544
11. ibid, 545
12. Caimbeul, M., A' *Càradh an Rathaid*, (Coiscéim), Dublin, 1988), 86
13. ibid, 88
14. Coveney, Dr P. and Highfield, Dr R., *The Arrow of Time*, (W. H. Allen, 1990), 292
15. Davies, Paul, *The Cosmic Blueprint*, (Penguin Books Ltd, London, 1995), 5
16., 17. & 18., ibid, pp 7, 5 & 3

Chapter 7

1. MacInnes, Dr John, *Dualchas nan Gàidheal*, Ed. Newton, J., (Birlinn, 2006), 459

Chapter 9

1. Jung, C. G., *Man and his Symbols*, (Aldous Books Ltd, London, 1964), 61
2. ibid, 61
3. Lennox, John C., *God's Undertaker: Has Science buried God?* (Lion, Oxford, 2007), 39
4. Caimbeul, M., *Saoghal Ùr*, (Diehard publishers, Callander, 2003), 20
5. Langemeijer, G. E., in the newspaper *Trouw*, October 6th, 1964
6. *Man and his Symbols*, 161–162

7. *New Testament*, Matthew, 16.26
8. ibid, John, 1.9

Chapter 10

1. Otto, Rudolph, translation of *Das Heilige* as *The Idea of the Holy*, (Oxford University Press, 1923), 7
2. Genesis, 18.27, King James Version
3. *The Idea of the Holy*, 28
4. *God's Undertaker: Has Science buried God?* 33 (see 3. Ch. 9)
5. *The Idea of the Holy*, 21
6. Caimbeul, M., *A' Gabhail Ris*, (Gairm, Glasgow, 1994), 38
7. *The Idea of the Holy*, 10
8. *New Writing Scotland 18*, (ASLS, 2001), 27
9. ibid, 25
10. *The Norton Anthology of English Literature*, (W. W. Norton & Company, Inc, New York, 1968), 1210

Chapter 11

1. *God's Undertaker: Has Science buried God?* 31 (see 3., Ch.8)
2. John, 14.6
3. John, 10.7–9
4. Romans, 1.20
5. ibid, 2.14–15
6. ibid, 9.30
7. John, 1.1–5
8. 1 Corinthians, 15.14
9. Montefiore, Hugh, *The Miracles of Jesus*, (SPCK, London, 2005), 2
10. ibid, 15
11. ibid, 109–110
12. ibid, 114
13. Habermas, Gary R., 'Jesus' Resurrection and Contemporary Criticism: An Apologetic (Part II)', *Criswell Theological Review 4.1* (Criswell College, 1989), 379
14. ibid, Part I, 163–169
15. *Collins English Dictionary*, (HarperCollins, 2005), 1033 & 1634

16. Varghese, R. A., The *Wonder of the World*, (Tyr Publishing, Fontain Hills, AZ, 2003), 23
17. ibid, 24
18. ibid, 24
19. Margenau, H. & Varghese, R. A., Eds, *Cosmos, Bios, Theos*, (Chicago & La Salle, 1992), 28
20. ibid, 33
21. ibid, 41
22. ibid, 111
23. Flew, Antony, *There is a God*, (HarperCollins, New York, 2007)

Chapter 12

1. Caimbeul, M., *Eileanan*, (Department of Celtic, University of Glasgow, 1980), 33
2. Ward, Keith, *God, Faith & the New Millennium*, (Oneworld, Oxford, 1998), 19
3. ibid, 43
4. ibid, 44
5. ibid, 35
6. ibid, 35
7. ibid, 36
8. Friesen, Dr J. Glenn http://www.members.shaw.ca/hermandooyeweerd/95Theses.html, 15–16
9. ibid, 15–16
10. *God, Faith & the New Millennium*, 48 (see 2. above)
11. ibid, 49

Chapter 15

1. Küng, Hans, *Does God Exist?* (Collins. London, 1980), 547
2. Collins, Francis, *The Language of God, A Scientist Presents Evidence for Belief*, (Pocket Books, London, 2007), 64
3. Rees, Martin, *Just Six Numbers*, (The Softback Review, London, 2000), 117–118
4. ibid, 66

5. Leslie, John, *The Prerequisites of Life in Our Universe*, (Truth Journal, 2009), 4
6. Rees, Martin, *Just Six Numbers*, 2 (see 3. above)
7. Friesen, Dr J. Glenn, (see Chapter 14, 8), 10
8. Schroeder, Gerald L., *The Hidden Face of God*, (Touchstone, New York, 2001), 40
9. ibid, 154
10. Davies, Paul, *The Fifth Miracle*, (Penguin Books, London, 1998), xviii
11. ibid, 256
12. ibid, 7
13. ibid, 71
14. ibid, 73
15. ibid, 100
16. ibid, 255–6
17. Collins, Francis, *The Language of God, A Scientist Presents Evidence for Belief* (Pocket Books, London, 2007), 225
18. ibid, 203
19. ibid, 201
20. Davies, Paul, The Fifth Miracle, Preface x.

Chapter 16

1. Acts, 17.28
2. Isaiah, 6.1–5

Chapter 17

1. Eliade, Mircea, *The Sacred and the Profane*, (Harcourt Books, Orlando, 1957), 17
2. Philippians, 2.6–11
3. Habermas, Gary R., *The Historical Jesus*, (College Press Publishing Company, Joplin), 145
4. Matthew, 18.21
5. ibid, 16.22–23

Chapter 18

1. Deuteronomy, 32.6
2. Isaiah, 63.16
3. John, 5.18
4. ibid, 14.9–10
5. ibid, 1.1
6. Lewis, C. S., *Essay Collection*, 'What are we to make of Jesus Christ?', (HarperCollins, London, 2002), 39
7. Mark, 1.15
8. Luke, 17.20–21
9. John, 3.6
10. John, 3.8
11. Philips, John A., *A Study of Bonhoeffer's Christology: The Form of Christ in the World*, (Collins, 1967), 241
12. Luke, 16.13
13. Job, 37.22
14. Psalm, 16.11
15. Exodus, 20.21
16. Joshua, 6.21
17. Joshua, 10.40
18. Jeremiah, 3.12
19. Daniel, 9.9
20. ibid, 9.4
21. Matthew, 4.44
22. John, 10.38
23. Matthew, 8.27
24. John, 1.2
25. ibid, 1.3
26. Jung, C. G., *Synchronicity, an Acausal connecting Principle*, (Ark Paperbacks, London, 1985), 91
27. Genesis, 12.3
28. John, 1.29
29. Micah, 5.2
30. John, 10.27–31

Chapter 19

1. Habermas Gary R., *The Case for the Resurrection of Jesus*, (Kregal Publications, Grand Rapids, 2004)
2. ibid, 47
3. ibid, 70
4. John, 14.6

Appendix

The following are the original Gaelic poems referred to / discussed in the foregoing text, followed by full English versions.

Plannt Mara

Is plannt mara mise
a chrathadh o chladaichean an t-saoghail.
Dh'fhaodte gun tachair sinn
(tha teans ann,
teans am measg iomadh teans)
am meadhan a' chuain,
gun deachaidh tusa cuideachd
àrach
ann an talamh Chalvin,
adhar ro Chopernicus os do chionn.

'S gun tàinig latha
nuair a thuit na reultan
's a bhrist an iarmailt na bloighean,
's gun do chaill thu do dhèantachd tìr',
air bhog
mi fhìn 's tu fhèin
tuilleadh
air maraichean fuara na falamhachd
gun fhreumh, gun iùil.

[from *Eileanan*, Glasgow, 1980]

Sea Plant

I'm a sea plant / shaken from the shores of the world. / Perhaps we'll meet / (there's a chance, / one among many) / in the middle of the ocean, / that you were also / raised / in Calvin's earth, / the pre-Copernican sky above you.

And the day came / when the stars fell / and the sky broke asunder, / and you lost your land-made form, / floating / you and I / forever more / on the cold empty seas / without root, without guide.

Gealach Shàmhach

Sinn anns
a' choille.
Os a cionn a' ghrian,
os a cionn a' ghealach.
Saoghal na grèine,
saoghal na gealaich,
aon a' losgadh,
an tèile fann.
Tha a' ghealach bàn
anns an aon adhar
anns a bheil na duilleagan a' tuiteam.
Nan glacainn a' ghealach bhàn
thuiteadh a' ghrian
nan glacainn an duilleag.

Fàilleadh puill
anns a' cheum dhonn,
an duilleag a' tuiteam
a rèir laghan na cruinne,
agus a' caochladh.
Tuitidh i gu sìorraidh,
a' sgaoileadh, a' ruigsinn aonachd.

An duilleag bhàn
anns a' pholl,
an eala bhàn air an tonn
agus a' ghrian gun sholas.

Dè 'm baile tha seo
a tha cho sàmhach?
An ainm an fhreastail
can rudeigin
mu aonachd, mu sgapadh.

Bhrist an duilleag na mìle pìos.
Cha tuirt a' ghealach guth.

[from *Bailtean*, Gairm, Glasgow, 1987]

Silent Moon

We / in the wood. / Above it the sun, / above it the moon. / Moon world, / sun world, / the one burning, / the one wan. / The moon is pale / in the same sky / in which the leaves are falling. / If I should catch the pale moon / the sun would fall / if I should catch the leaf.

Mud smell / in the brown path, / the leaf falling / according to nature's laws, / and dying. / It will fall forever, / dispersing, uniting.

The pale leaf / in the mud, the white swan on the wave / and the sun without light.

What town is this / that is so silent? / For God's sake / say something / about unity, about scattering.

The leaf broke in a thousand pieces. / The moon was silent.

Sùil air ais

Dà fhichead bliadhna 's mi dall fhathast,
gun freagairt agam ('s cha bhi)
dha ceistean mòra na cruinne –
's an dèidh sin chan eil ann ach iad,
ged 's tric a bheir sinn ar car asainn fhìn
nuair a chì sinn latha mar an-diugh –
fionnar, brèagha, 's a' ghrian ag òradh talamh,
glasach, sràid-thaighean is bàgh.
'S lùiginn an uair sin nach robh ceist ann
mar ceist a' bhàis, no ceist na fìrinn,
no dè tha Gràdh, Dia, Crìosd a' ciallachadh,
agus mìle nì eile nach fosgail tuigse,
gus am bi mo cheann na chuairt-shruth –
ach thig mi air ais, agus air ais a-rithist,
nam shlige-bhàt'.

Smaoinich mi uair gun robh freagairt ann,
gun tuiteadh meas o chraoibh an eòlais
's gun ithinn ubhal a' ghliocais, no gu labhradh guth
le ùghdarras dè nach gabhadh àicheadh
on mheall teine. Càil ach sàmhachd.
Càil ach mìorbhail an dèidh mìorbhail
mar a dh'fheumas duine aideachadh
a ghabhas beachd air Nàdar no air atam
dhe stuth na cruinne, ach uile nàdarrach, reusanta,
gu ìre. 'S e bha mi 'g iarraidh ach trombaid, teine,
a dhearbhadh gu robh nì tuigseach ann
taobh thall na sgàile. Chan eil an saoghal
no Dia (às bith dè an seòrsa bith a th'ann)
ag obrachadh mar sin. Càil ach sàmhachd –
's faireachdainn nach gabh a chur am facail
gu bheil nithean ann nach eil ag iarraidh bruidhinn,
's a tha, 's nach eil buileach a' ruighinn oirnn

leis nach eil iad a' bruidhinn nar cainnt.
Aon latha thig iad, 's dòcha, a' taomadh
a-mach às adhar air choreigin.
Ach mus tachair sin bidh sinne 's dòcha coma,
coma co-aca.

[from *A' Càradh an Rathaid*, Dublin, 1988]

Looking Back

*Forty and still blind / without an answer (and I never will
have) / for the universal questions / – despite these being all there
is, / although we often deceive ourselves / when we see a day
like today / fresh, bright, and the sun gilding the earth, / grass,
street and bay. I'd wish then there weren't such questions, / as
the question of death, truth, / or what Love, God, Christ means, /
and a thousand other things undisclosed, / until my brain is a
whirlpool – / but I return, and return again / in my shell of a boat.*

*I thought once there was an answer, / that fruit would fall from the
tree of knowledge / and that I'd eat the apple of wisdom, or that
a voice would speak / with undeniable authority / from the pillar
of fire. Nothing but silence. / Nothing but miracle after miracle /
as anybody must confess / who considers Nature or one atom /
of the world's material, but all natural, reasonable, / to an extent.
What I wanted was a trumpet, a fire, / which would prove there
was something intelligent / beyond the veil. / The world / or God
(whatever kind of being it is) / doesn't work like that. Nothing but
silence – / and a feeling that cannot be expressed / that there are
things that want to speak, / and that do, and do not quite reach us /
because they don't speak our language.*

*They will come one day, perhaps, pouring / out of some sky. / But
before that happens perhaps we won't care / not care at all.*

An Craiceann ùr

Tha an da-rìribh seo orm
mar chom, mar cheann,
mar chraiceann drùidhteach ùr –
flinne neo-fhaicsinneach
gam bhogadh gum smior.
Nuair a thòisicheas a' chrith
cha dèan an còmhdach seo feum,
's chan eil stuth eile ann
a chruthaich dia
a dhèanadh fear eile.

[from *A' Gabhail Ris*, Glasgow, 1994]

New Skin

This reality surrounds me / like a body, a head, / a new pervasive skin – an invisible sleet / soaking me to the core. When the trembling starts / this covering will be useless, / and there is no / god-created material / to make another.

Luinneagan bho Nàmhaid na Sìthe*

1

Tha sinn mar aislingean a sheasas
bliadhna no dhà – aislingean ag
aisling aisling. Cò ris a dh'fheitheas
an saoghal teinnteach no an t-sradag?
Cainnt dhinn, dhe ar n-eanchainn,
mar chuibhreann, sinne de chainnt.
Lasraichean ann an teine sinn,
gar lasadh agus loisgte ann.
An aisling as baoithe uile –
toglaichean faoine nam facal,
far am faic iomadach duine

lùchairt ghlòrmhor far nach eil càil.
Tha thu a-nis am meadhan aisling,
am meadhan fhacal dàin lasraich.

* 'Nàmhaid na Sìthe' – i.e., reusan

[from *A' Gabhail Ris*, Glasgow, 1994]

(from) Ditties from the Enemy of Peace*

1

*We are dreams which last / a year or two – dreams / dreaming
dreams. What will / assuage the fiery world or the spark? /
Language of us, of our brain, / a part, we of language. / We are
flames in a fire, / lighting us and burnt in it. / The silliest dream of
all – / the vain contructions of words, / where many a person will
see / a glorious palace where there is nothing. / You are now in the
middle of a dream, / in the midst of a flaming poem.*

* the Enemy of Peace – i.e., reason

An Kaleidoscope

Chuir mi mo shùil ris an lionsa
a choimhead nam pàtran ioma-dhathte,
saoghal mìorbhaileach air a chumadh
's a' falbh cha mhòr mus fhaict' e.

Na dathan uile an deagh òrdugh,
òirdheirc ann an aiteas laghail,
mar na rionnagan fuar san adhar
gun aon fhaireachdainn gan tadhal.

Le mùthadh beag na làimhe
cruthaichidh mi saoghail ùra;
tuitidh na lannan mar fhaileas,
chì mi gu bheil gach nì nam shùilean –

solais ag èirigh am pàtran,
an inntinn a' cur a camadh fhèin orr',
gun nì ann ach pàtran san t-sùil
agus pàtrain a' briseadh gun feum orr'.

Falamhachd an dathan luaisgte,
's e MacGill-Eain uair a chunnaic
's e faicinn a' chorra-ghrithich
a' sireadh lòin mar nì an duine;

beo airson tiotan san t-solas
mar phàtran prìseil no falamh,
a' dol dhan uaigh fhuar sgriosail,
a' dol gu sìorraidh à sealladh.

[from *A' Gabhail Ris*, Glasgow, 1994]

The Kaleidoscope

I placed my eye to the lens / to watch the multi-coloured patterns, / a wonderful world created / and disappearing almost before it is visible.

The colours perfectly ordered, / splendid in organised joy, / like the chill stars in the sky / strangers to a single feeling.

With a slight hand movement / I create new worlds; / the scales fall like a shadow, / I recognise that everything is in my vision –

lights forming in a pattern, / the mind giving them its own slant, / nothing there but a pattern in the eye / and patterns dissolving uselessly.

Emptiness in mobile colours, / as MacLean once perceived / as he noticed a heron / seeking food as a human does;

alive for a moment in the light / as a precious or empty pattern, / entering the cold deplorable grave, / going eternally from sight.

A' Càradh an Rathaid

Oilisgin buidh' orm
's mi càradh an rathaid,
a' lìonadh nan toll
le teàrr agus morghan.
Tha cuimhn' a' m mar a bha an teàrr
a' bristeadh na bhuilgein
ann an teas na h-òige.
Sinn a-nise
a' càradh an rathaid
nach eil a' dol a dh'àite.

Thàinig fear a thuirt:
Cuir an siud i, a charaid –
tha an rathad a' bristeadh for casan.
Teàrr a' chridhe fàs cruaidh,
gun ghrian ann ga thòcadh,
e dìreadh, e teàrnadh,
's gun teàrnadh ann-
an t-aon a dhèanadh feum.

Eun air a' ghèig
's e seinn leis fhèin:
Ille bhig, ille bhig,
na biodh dragh ort,
na biodh dragh ort,
chan eil rathad anns an adhar,
carson a tha thu a' càradh
an rathaid nach eil a' dol a dh'àite?

Tha an rathad cho cùilteach,
gluasadach, lùbach,
fo fhàire fradhairc,
na lìon-chuislean gun chrìch
ann am bodhaig na cruinne,

aon mhionaid cho slàn
's an uair sin ga phronnadh.

Na creid, na creid
nach eil e dol a dh'àite
(arsa bodach an rathaid);
abaichidh gach nì
's bidh an cridhe sàsaicht'
le samhla,
le fuil bhlàth nan cuislean
's thig gach nì gu àite
mar anns an toiseach.

An-dràsta lìon na tuill
's bi dol air d' aghaidh:
feumaidh gach duine bhith siubhal –
's a' càradh.

[from *A' Càradh an Rathaid*, Dublin, 1988]

Mending the road

With a yellow oilskin on / I mend the road, / and fill the holes / with tar and gravel. / I remember the tar / how the bubbles would break / in the heat of youth. / Now we / mend the road / that goes nowhere.

A man came who said: / Put it there, my friend – / the road breaks beneath our feet. / The heart's tar hardens, / no sun to swell it. / It decends and climbs – / there is no ascent/salvation – / the only one for remedy.

A bird on the twig / singing by itself: little boy, little boy, / don't worry, / don't worry, / there is no road in the sky, / why do you mend / the road that goes nowhere?

The road is so devious / mobile, tortuous, / hidden from view, / the endless vein-webs / in the body of creation, / one moment so whole / and the next in smithereens.

Don't believe, don't believe / that it goes nowhere / (said the old man of the road); / everything will ripen / and the heart will be satisfied / with a symbol, / with the arteries' warm blood / and everything will arrive in its place / as in the beginning.

For now, fill the holes / and go forward: / everyone must travel/ pass on – / and be mending.

Dhutsa, Fhìrinn – cò dha eile?

1

An toiseach 's mi òg
bha mi smaoineachadh
gum faighinn thu gu cinnteach.

Thàinig thu a-rithist
ann an riochd maighdinn –
carson a' ghàire?

Thu ioma-chruthach.
Chan fhaca mi ach
do chùl a' dol à sealladh.

A! a ghràidh,
tha thu fad-shiùbhlach,
a' bruidhinn ann am mìle riochd.

2

Gach nì na shiabann
air muir chaoir-uamhannach
a' dol à sealladh.

A' chreag fhèin
na siabann leis an nigh mi m' aodann –
cho neo-mhaireannach.

A h-uile flùra na sheasamh
ag ràdh
gur esan thusa.

3

Tha pàirt dhìot aig na h-uile
's chan eil thu uile
aig duine.

An t-amadan cinnteach
g' eil thu aige:
thusa a bhuilgein mhaisich!

E nise na chleasaiche
le aghaidh choimheach –
mar gum biodh sibh co-ionann.

A dhreach sòlaimt',
uil'-fhiosrach; cha mhòr
nach creidinn gu robh thu aige.

4

An t-aon air cùl na h-aisling?
Chan eil fhios a'm.
Tha an cùirtear air chrith.

[from *A' Càradh an Rathaid*, Dublin, 1988]

For you, Truth – for whom else?

1

At first, when young / I thought / I would find you for sure.
You appeared again / in feminine form – / why the laughter?
Multiform. / All I saw / was your back disappearing.
Ah! Darling, / you are far-travelled, / speaking a thousand tongues.

2

Everything froth / on a raging sea / going out of sight.
The rock itself / a soap/foam to wash my face – / so fleeting.
Every flower stands / claiming / it is you.

3

Everyone possesses a part of you / and no-one / has all of you.
The fool certain / that he has you: / you, you lovely bubble!
Now a clown / with a falseface – / as if you were equal/the same.
His appearance solemn, / all-knowing; I should almost / believe he
*   possessed you.*

4

The one behind the dream? / I've no idea. / The veil trembles.

Na còig Gnèthean

Is mise am feòlmhor, air mo shlìobadh le miann,
itealag dhian, suas is sìos anns an stoirm;
chan fhaigh mi air falbh bho làmh ìseal an diabhail.

Is mise an reusanta, a dh'fheumas bhith caomh;
tha an saoghal ag iarraidh nach strìochd sinn dhan bhèist –
cùm ris an riaghailt 's bidh sonas leat is maoin.

Is mise am moralta, tha dleastanas sgrìobht' air mo chàil;
tha iarrtas fo chuing, is grod leam ana-miann is aimhreit;
tha leabhar nan riaghailt a' gleidheadh ar beatha bhon ghràisg.

Is mise mac an iomfhios, tha doimhneachd nam rèim;
mic is nigheanan Dhè sinn, is clann an deagh bheus;
feumar bhith umhail, le gràdh is urram dha chèil'.

Is mise an dìomhair, choinnich mi am Bith th' air cùl fèin;
tha fiamh is uamharr' is aiteas nam shnuadh;
chunnaic is dh'fhairich mi slànachd nan reul.

[from *Saoghal Ùr*, Callander, 2003]

The five Natures

I'm the flesh, stroked by desire, / a wanton kite, up and down in the storm; / I can't escape the devil's low grasp.

I'm the rational, who has to be decent; / the world requires we don't yield to the beast; / keep to the rule and you'll have happiness and wealth.

I'm the moral, duty is written on my heart; / desire is subjugated, I detest lust and discord; / keeping the rules saves our lives from the mob.

I'm intuition's progeny, governed by depth, / sons and daughters of God, of best conduct; / we must be obedient, loving and honouring each other.

I'm the mystic, who has met the Being behind self; / awe and dread are in my face; / I've seen and felt the wholeness of the stars.

Òran

Chunna mi a ghrian ag èirigh
mar bhall neochiontach sna speuran ...
Sèist:
's thòisich an t-uamhann tighinn orm.

Chunna mi na h-eòin bheaga
mar a tha iad cho seòlta a' freagairt ...

Chunna mi mar bha do ghaol dhomh
ged nach tuiginn e daonnan ...

Chunna mi na daoine mòra
mar a bha iad a' marbhadh an seòrsa ...

Chunna mi nach fhaighinn thuigsinn
ged bhithinn air ceud a ruigsinn ...

Chunna mi an t-seasmhachd uamhraidh
a tha an ataman na stuaghan ...

Chunna mi nach eil san t-sàl dhubh
faireachdainn son neach a bhàthar ...

Chunna mi an t-astar cianail
air an tèid solas san iarmailt ...

Chunna mi am briseadh dùile
a thèid fhulang gun sùil ris ...

Chunna mi thu shaoghal nan gràsan
a' tionndadh mar leug san fhànas ...

Chuimhnich mi mar thuirt an Sgriobtar,
eagal Dhè toiseach gliocais ...

[from *A' Gabhail Ris*, Glasgow, 1994]

Song

I saw the sun rising / like an innocent globe in the sky ...

Chorus: and I was seized with dread/awe.

I saw the little birds / with their skilful responses ...

I saw how you loved me / although I didn't always understand it ...

I saw the adults / how they killed their own kind ...

I saw I could never fathom it / although I lived to be a hundred ...

I saw the fearful stability / in the atoms of the waves ...

I saw that in the dark brine / there is no feeling for the drowned ...

I saw the incredible speed / of light travelling through space ...

I saw the distress / suffered unexpectedly ...

I saw you, world of graces / turning like a jewel in space ...

I remembered what Scripture said, / the fear of God, the beginning of wisdom ...

A' Bhoiteag

1

Nam bhoiteig
ann an ùir an t-saoghail,
bidh mi, saoilidh mì, a' faireachdainn blàths
mar gum biodh làmh gam shuathadh.
Uaireannan os mo chionn
bidh mi a' faireachdainn coiseachd
gun fhosadh
gun lasadh,
ach aon latha

mar gun dùisgeadh rudeigin an ùir
chaidh mo shadail suas
agus loisg soillse gun ainm mo chùl.

B' fheàrr leam gun robh mi
air ais anns an ùir
a' faireachdainn na corraig caoin
gam bhuaireadh
gam shuathadh
le eòlas an t-solais àird, àrd os mo chionn.

2

Faodaidh a' bhoiteag fhèin
cuideam an dè fhaireachdainn.

Faodaidh a' bhoiteag fhèin
blàths na grèin aithneachadh.

[from *Saoghal Ùr*, Callander, 2003]

The Worm

1

A worm / in the soil of the world, / I sometimes, I think, feel a warmth / as if a hand were stroking me. / Sometimes above me / I feel footsteps / without pause, / ceaseless, / but one day / as if something disturbed the soil / I was thrown upwards / and an unknown glow burnt my back.

I wish I was / back in the soil / feeling the gentle finger / agitating me / stroking me / with the knowledge of the distant light, high above me.

2

Even the worm / can feel the weight of the god.

Even the worm / can recognise the heat of the sun.

Briseadh na Cloiche

Thog thu còmhnaidh, a Ghlòir,
nam chridhe
's gun fhios a'm gun robh thu ga thogail.
O iongantais neo-fhaicsinnich an spioraid!
Am measg a' chlàbair 's a' phuill
bha do làmhan
ro gheal
ag ullachadh an làraich,
nì do-thuigsinn
nach gabh tuigsinn
nach gabh creidsinn.
A! Tha a' chlach seo fhathast
gad chumail a-mach,
bruid mhòr far am bu chòir staran a bhith.

Bris i, a Ghlòir,
ged a bhiodh e goirt, bris i
na bloighdean beaga
gus am bi slighe rèidh ann, mu dheireadh,
dhad chois
agus cluinnidh mi fuaim do choise air
a' ghreabhail
agus bidh mi le fiamh 's le uamhann
a' feitheamh glòir do theachd.

'S bidh an taigh a bha falamh
làn de àirneis iongantach.
làn, làn, làn,
agus na neoni.

[from *Saoghal Ùr*, Callander, 2003]

The Breaking of the Stone

You built a dwelling, Glory, / in my heart, / although unaware you were building it. / O invisible marvel of the spirit! / In the midst of the mire and mud / your hands / most white / were preparing the site / something inexplicable / inscrutable / unbelievable.

Ah! The stone is still there / keeping you out, / a great brute of a stone where a path should be.

*Break it, Glory, / although painful, break it / in smithereens / until there is a smooth path, at last, / for your foot / and I will hear the sound of your feet on the gravel
and with awe and dread / I'll wait your glorious arrival.*

And the once empty house / will be full of amazing furniture, / full, full, full, / and it will be nothing.

Index

THE ISLANDS BOOK TRUST – high quality books on
island themes in English and Gaelic

Based in Lewis, the Islands Book Trust are a charity committed to furthering understanding and appreciation of the history of Scottish islands in their wider Celtic and Nordic context. We do this through publishing books, organising talks and conferences, visits, radio broadcasts, research and education on island themes. For details of membership of the Book Trust, which will keep you in touch with all our publications and other activities, see www.theislandsbooktrust.com or phone 01851 880737.

The Islands Book Trust
Ravenspoint
Kershader
South Lochs
Isle of Lewis
HS2 9QA

Tel: 01851 880737

www.theislandsbooktrust.com